DEFENDING ANIMAL RIGHTS

Defending Animal Rights

TOM REGAN

UNIVERSITY OF ILLINOIS PRESS

URBANA AND CHICAGO

Library of Congress Cataloging-in-Publication Data
Regan, Tom.
Defending animal rights / Tom Regan.
p.   cm.
Includes bibliographical references and index.
ISBN 0-252-02611-X (cloth : alk. paper)
1. Animal rights—Philosophy.
2. Animal welfare—Moral and ethical aspects.
I. Title.
HV4711.R366   2001
179.3—dc21   00–008708

C 5 4 3 2 1

*To Jane Cullen,
mentor, friend*

In a democracy, only those who speak up are heard.
—Marvin Harris

Animals, who we have made our slaves, we do not like to regard as our equals.
—Charles Darwin

The end of man is an action, not a thought.
—Thomas Carlyle

CONTENTS

PREFACE

The present volume collects some of the work I have done during the last decade; individually and collectively the several chapters give some sense of where my thought has led me during this period. "Animal rights" is the unifying theme. What does this idea mean? How does it differ from animal welfare? How is it related to animal liberation? Why think animals have rights? What are the main objections to thinking that they do? Philosophical questions, one and all; each is taken up in one or more of the nine chapters, always, I think, in ways not found in my work published a decade ago.

Some of the chapters situate animal rights outside a strictly philosophical context. The last two chapters address personal and professional dimensions of advocacy. Chapter 8 ("Ivory Towers Should Not a Prison Make") explores challenges academic philosophers can face when they act as advocates for a cause, and chapter 9 ("Work, Hypocrisy, and Integrity") asks how employees, including academicians, can make moral sense of remaining "on the job" when they believe that their employers are engaged in immoral practices. As an animal rights advocate who works at a university where thousands of animals are killed every year, and where some faculty have not taken kindly to counting me among their professional peers, both chapters involve issues that have arisen in my own life. But issues of both types can arise for anyone who advocates changes in the status quo.

In addition to chapters addressing the philosophical, the personal, and the professional, two chapters place the idea of animal rights in a larger historical context. Chapter 6 ("Patterns of Resistance") examines some of the justifications science and religion have offered in defense of the worst forms of social inequality (for example, denying basic rights to gays and lesbians) and looks for parallels between these defenses, on the one hand, and scientific and religious justifications of humanity's tyranny over other animals, on the other. Chapter 7 ("Understanding Animal Rights Violence") examines some of the similarities between today's animal rights movement and the nineteenth-century movement to abolish slavery as a way to understand why the use of violence by animal rights advocates is as predictable as it is regrettable.

Differ though the chapters do, whether in subject matter or approach, each attempts to find its place within the larger mosaic that is animal rights, now viewed from one angle, now another. Most were originally read as invited lectures, either for professional audiences, for gatherings of animal rights advocates, or for the general public. Each is accompanied by a short introduction that explains the specific details of its initial presentation: the why, where, when, and for whom. All have been edited with a view to making them less like public lectures to be heard and more like essays to be read. I have also tried to minimize the amount of repetition that inevitably occurs when the same person writes about closely related ideas on different occasions. I hope these modifications help make the collection more "reader friendly." Still, no amount of editorial tinkering alters the truth of the thoughts expressed. Understandably, it is the substance of what the words written here say, more than the style in which they say it, that matters most to me.

Gratitude I owe and, in the pages that follow, express to many, adding here a special thanks to Richard Wentworth and Bruce Bethell, both of the University of Illinois Press, the former for his encouragement and the latter for his editorial assistance. If I have neglected properly to acknowledge my debts to anyone, I sincerely hope the omission will be understood as resulting from my fallible memory, not the narrowness of my sense of indebtedness. I view myself as incredibly (and, beyond any question, undeservedly) blessed. I am fully aware that the ideas I advocate go against the grain of the dominant culture in which we find ourselves. At other times, in other places, people have been severely punished for publicly avowing ideas less "heretical" than mine. I have my share of moral briefs to file against America, past and present, as do many others, but the extent to which this nation lets its dissenters express their beliefs freely is one of history's crowning achievements. That I enjoy this freedom is just one dimension of my moral luck.

Many are the obstacles standing in the way of animal liberation. Too few are the partisans committed to the cause; too many, those comfortable with the culture of oppression. The struggle for animal rights is not for the faint of heart. I hope these pages play some role, however small, in helping make life better for other-than-human animals—and for those who are human, too.

DEFENDING ANIMAL RIGHTS

1

ETHICAL THEORY AND ANIMALS

Few areas of applied philosophy have witnessed more dramatic growth in the recent past than has bioethics; moreover, given the pace of advances in the life sciences, from developments in preventive medicine to the cloning of sheep and mice, few areas of ethical concern are likely to grow more dramatically in the foreseeable future. Depending on one's perspective, humanity is either on the borders of a new world that promises a harvest of hitherto undreamed of benefits, populated by compassionate Dr. Spocks and Dr. Welbys, or poised on the sharp precipice of our worst nightmares, peopled with the good doctors Frankenstein and Moreau. Whatever the future holds, one thing is certain: other-than-human animals will be used in the name of advancing scientific knowledge, both basic and applied. What is less certain is whether in doing so, those who use them will act wisely and well.

Although people of goodwill can and often do disagree in the answers they give to questions about the morality of using animals for scientific purposes, virtually everyone agrees that these are legitimate and inescapable ethical questions. Near unanimity on this point is a recent phenomenon. Less than a hundred years ago, the distinguished American neurologist Charles Loomis Dana argued that animal advocates suffer from a mental illness; zoophil-psychosis (love-of-animals psychosis), he called it. Dana's diagnosis cast long shadows. As late as the 1960s, opponents of the U.S. Animal Welfare Act sometimes charged that the act's advocates suffered from this type of insanity. Even as recently as 1990, another neurosurgeon, Robert J. White, declared that "animal usage is not a moral or ethical issue and elevating the problem of animal rights to such a plane is a disservice to medical research and the farm and dairy industry" (1990:43). (These matters are discussed more fully in chapter 6.)

1

White's view is remarkable because it is so out of step with the near consensus mentioned previously. One symptom of the growing acceptance that animal usage *is* a moral or ethical issue is found in comprehensive works in bioethics, which now include discussions of *animal rights* and *animal welfare*, but none for *zoophil-psychosis*. And these topics appear not merely in books on the margins of respectability; today they occupy a place of prominence in the most respected resource works in the field, including the *Encyclopedia of Bioethics*, where the present chapter first appeared.

In the invitation I received to contribute to the 1993 edition of the encyclopedia, I was asked to write an entry that would serve as "the anchor for the series of articles in the entry on Animal Welfare and Rights and . . . as an introduction to the issues that will be discussed throughout the entry." The issues to be discussed included vegetarianism, wildlife and conservation management, domestic animals and pets, zoos and zoological parks, hunting, and animals in agriculture and factory farming. In addition, a three-article entry on animal research was planned. All this occurred just a decade after the first edition of the encyclopedia, whose only entry devoted to nonhuman animals was a two-part, seven-page discussion of animal research. So, yes, times do change—sometimes. Remarkably, the only entry for *animal* in the 1998 *Cambridge Dictionary of Philosophy* is "animal faith," a concept used by the American philosopher George Santayana that has absolutely nothing to do with the moral status of animals.

In any event, my task in accepting the assignment for the *Encyclopedia of Bioethics*, as I conceived it, was to write an overview of the animal rights debate, broadly conceived—to describe, that is, the main positions taken by those who have written on the relevant topics and to explain how the moral status of nonhuman animals plays an increasingly vital role in the assessment of competing ethical theories. Telling the complete story was out of the question, but it seemed possible to offer a reasonably full account, one that ranged from Aristotle, who addressed these matters thousands of years ago, to representative advocates of ecofeminism and deep ecology, who put pen to paper "yesterday," so to speak. A fuller elaboration and partial defense of the position I favor—what I call "the rights view"—is offered in the next two chapters.

Originally published as "Animal Welfare and Rights: Ethical Perspectives on the Treatment and Status of Nonhuman Animals," in *The Encyclopedia of Bioethics*, rev. ed., ed. Warren T. Reich (New York: Macmillan, 1993). Reprinted with the permission of the publisher.

❖

Normative ethical theory may be conceived as the systematic inquiry into the moral limits on human freedom. Philosophers and theologians throughout history and across cultures have offered different, often contradictory answers to the central question of ethics thus conceived. Some have argued, for example, that the only justified limits on human freedom are those grounded in an agent's rational self-interest, whereas others have maintained that the foundations of morality, and thus the basis of morally justified limitations on human freedom, are logically distinct from self-interest, though not from the dictates of reason. Still others have alleged that the foundations of morality have nothing to do with either reason or self-interest.

In view of the variety and conflicting nature of answers to the central question of normative ethics, it is hardly surprising that ethical theories sometimes offer strikingly different accounts of the moral status of those nonhuman animals we humans raise or hunt for food and clothing, use as beasts of burden, train to entertain us, and utilize as models in biomedical research. No philosopher or theologian has gone so far as to say that, from the moral point of view, there are no justified limits on what we may do to these animals. Even René Descartes, much celebrated for his theory that nonhuman animals are automata and thus incapable of feeling either pain or pleasure (Descartes 1976), is said to have treated his dog humanely. At a certain minimal level, then, all normative ethical theories speak with one voice. At other levels, however, the differences are both real and deep.

Direct and Indirect Duties

These differences clearly emerge when we consider how competing theories answer two distinct but related questions. First, what are the grounds for morally limiting human freedom when it comes to human interactions with nonhuman animals? Second, how extensive are these moral limits on human freedom? The former asks why human freedom should be limited at all when our actions affect other animals; the latter challenges us to investigate how much our freedom should be limited. The first question is the more basic, since the reasons given in support of views about the extent of our freedom ultimately rest on views about reasons for limiting our freedom in the first place.

Two opposed possibilities present themselves as answers to the first, more basic question. One possibility holds that we should limit our freedom because of the ways *animals themselves* are affected or treated by human agents. Viewed from this perspective, nonhuman animals themselves are entitled to a certain kind of consideration or treatment. Because such views stress the idea that something is owed or due directly to animals, it is common to refer to them as *direct* duty views.

The second possibility locates the ground of moral constraint in some basis other than the animals themselves. Viewed from this perspective, humans owe nothing to other animals, nor do these animals themselves deserve any sort of treatment or consideration. Rather, human freedom should be limited because, for example, human cruelty to other animals will cause humans to treat one another cruelly. Because such views deny that we have duties directly to other animals, while recognizing that other factors should limit our freedom in our dealings with them, they are commonly referred to as *indirect* duty views.

All normative ethical theories, as they address the moral status of nonhuman animals, fall into one or the other of these two classes. That is, either they affirm that we have direct duties to nonhuman animals, or they deny that we have direct duties. Some of the major theoretical options within each class, as these have been developed by ethicists within the history of Western thought, will be considered in what follows.

Abolition, Reform, and the Status Quo

As noted earlier, a second important question asks how much our freedom should be limited in our dealings with other animals. Three sorts of options may be distinguished: abolition, reform, and the status quo. An abolitionist position argues on behalf of ending human practices that routinely utilize nonhuman animals (for example, as a source of food or as models in scientific research). A reformist position accepts these institutions in principle but seeks in various ways to improve them in practice (for example, by enlarging cage sizes for animals used in research). A status-quo position, unlike the abolitionist one, accepts these institutions in principle and, unlike the reformist stance, does not recognize the need to improve them. Representative examples of each outlook and their logical relationship to competing normative ethical theories will be explained in the following subsections.

While the heated, sometimes acrimonious debate among partisans of abolition, reform, and the status quo captures the attention of the media, far less attention has been devoted to critical assessment of the competing ethical philosophies, whether of the direct or indirect duty variety. This by itself suggests the degree to which the public debate over "animal rights," broadly conceived, has assumed the greater part of the issue most in need of informed, critical reflection. Clearly, deciding whether we should favor the goals of abolition, reform, or the status quo in practice depends on determining the most adequate account concerning how we should treat non-human animals in theory. It is to a consideration of some of the major options in ethical theory that I now turn.

Perfectionism

Aristotle ("Animals and Slavery," 1976) presents the broad outlines of a moral theory called *perfectionism*. The cornerstone of this theory has a high degree of initial plausibility. Justice, it is claimed, consists in giving to individuals what they are due, and those individuals whose characters are morally better (more nearly "perfect") than the characters of others prima facie deserve more of what is good in life than do other, less good people. Aristotle's accounts of what makes people morally better and of "the good of Man" have helped shape much of Western moral theory. Concerning the latter, Aristotle accepts the commonplace notion that the good we humans seek is happiness, but he argues that the true happiness we seek is not abundant wealth, fame, or even pleasure but rather the possession and exercise of those virtues (or "excellencies") that are uniquely human. Thus happiness, in his view, is "an activity of the soul in accordance with virtue." Those are happiest who optimally express their humanity in *the ways they live* and, in doing so, take pleasure in being the human beings they are.

As for the moral virtues (prudence, justice, courage, and temperance), Aristotle characterizes each as a mean between the two extremes of excess and deficiency. A courageous person, for example, is neither foolhardy (an excess) nor cowardly (a deficiency); a courageous person has the right mix of the willingness to take risks and the fear of doing so. Among the intellectual virtues, the highest is a detached, contemplative wisdom, wherein one knows eternal truths and in this way shares in that knowledge possessed by the gods. Finally, in the case of both the moral and the intellectual virtues, the human capacity to reason plays a decisive role. For man is, in Aristotle's view, unique in being "a rational animal," and "the good of man" consists in actualizing, to the fullest extent possible, those unique potentialities that define what it is to be human. Thus, since those who optimally express their humanity in their actions are the happiest, the happiest people are those who exercise their reason optimally.

Because it prescribes distributing what is good in life on the basis of one's possessing the favored virtues and thus according to degrees of human perfection, perfectionism can—and in Aristotle's hands, does—sanction or require radically inegalitarian treatment of different individuals. In the case of nonhuman animals in particular, perfectionism provides no direct protection. Although Aristotle (in sharp contrast to Descartes) asserts that these animals share with humans many of the same psychological capacities, including, for example, sensation and desire, he confidently denies that they share the capacity to reason. Moreover, because in his view the "lesser" exists to serve the interests or purposes of the "greater," Aristotle maintains that nonhuman animals exist for the purpose of advancing the good of human beings. He writes: "Other animals exist for the sake of man, the tame for use and food, the wild, if not all, at least the greater part of them, for food, and for the provision of clothing and various instruments" (Aristotle 1976:110). There is no implication here that Aristotle's teachings permit the wanton infliction of pain on nonhuman animals for no good reason. What is clear is that because he recognizes no purpose for nonhuman animals greater than serving the interests of human beings, he can recognize only indirect duties in their case. Finally, while many of today's more controversial practices involving human utilization of nonhuman animals, such as factory farming and animal-to-human organ transplants, were unknown in his day, all the available evidence seems to indicate that Aristotle was well disposed to the status quo with respect to the relevant practices current while he was alive.

It is not only nonhuman animals, however, who exist for the sake of those who are more perfect. In general, women do not measure up to Aristotle's standards of "the good of man." "The male is by nature superior, and the female inferior," he writes, "and the one rules, and the other is ruled; this principle, of necessity, extends to all mankind" (Aristotle 1976:110). In addition some humans, whether male or female, lack the ability to grasp through reason those truths understood by the more virtuous among us; such individuals are "slave[s] by nature" (ibid.). Aristotle thus affirms the obvious parallel between the moral status of human slaves and that of nonhuman animals: "The use made of slaves and of tame animals is not very different; for both with their bodies minister to the needs of life" (ibid.). Those humans who, because of their superior rationality, are morally more perfect are entitled to make use of those, whether human or not, who lack the virtues defining human perfection.

Few today will publicly embrace Aristotelian perfectionism. Not only does his view of women offend the emancipated gender egalitarianism of our time, but the comfortable elitism and classism that enable him to pronounce some humans slaves "by nature" find no home among the most basic precepts of contemporary moral, political, and legal thought. The practical implications of Aristotelian perfectionism's fundamental principle—namely, that those who are lacking in reason exist to serve the interests of those who are most virtuous—are morally offensive. It is one thing to affirm that people who possess greater capacities prima facie deserve more of what is good in life; it is quite another to maintain that those who possess lesser ones exist for the sole purpose of ministering to the more virtuous. If the argument fails to justify exploitation of "less virtuous" humans, then there is little reason to suppose it will justify exploitation of animals. Arguably, consistency requires that if we disallow the one kind of exploitation, we must disallow the other.

Despotism and Stewardship

One alternative to Aristotle's philosophy is rooted in the Judeo-Christian biblical teaching that God gives human beings dominion over nature in general and other animals in particular. As so often happens, however, there is more than one way to interpret the biblical message. Two ways in which human dominion can be understood—as despotism or stewardship—will be sketched here.

Despotism teaches that nature in general and the other animals in particular are created by God for the sake of humans; they are thus ordained by the divine creator to serve myriad human purposes, for example, by being a source of food and clothing. Only humans have intrinsic value; the natural world possesses value only to the extent that it serves human interests. In this sense, human interests are the measure of all things, at least all things of value. Various biblical passages are cited to confirm the despotic reading, for example, "Then God said, 'Let us make man in our image, after our likeness; and let them have dominion over the fish of the sea, and over the birds of the air, and over the cattle, and over all the earth'" (Gen. 1:26).

Seen in this light, despotism's appeal to what God has ordained provides a reason for human supremacy over nonhuman animals that appears to be absent from Aristotle's appeal to what is guaranteed "by nature," and it is a small step from accepting the despotic interpretation of human dominion to concluding that we owe nothing to nonhuman animals themselves. Thus St. Thomas Aquinas, for example, adds a reference to God to words otherwise barely distinguishable from those of Aristotle, asserting that it is by "divine ordinance that the life of animals and plants is preserved not for themselves but for man" (Aquinas 1976:119). Mindful, moreover, that some biblical passages prohibit cruelty to nonhuman animals, Aquinas firmly places himself within the indirect duty tradition when he maintains that the import of such prohibitions is, for example, "to remove man's thoughts from being cruel to other men, and lest through being cruel to animals one become cruel to human beings" (Aquinas 1976:59).

To the extent that St. Thomas's philosophy is rooted in the Scripture of the Christian tradition, those who stand outside this tradition are unlikely to be persuaded that God established in nature what nature was incapable of establishing by itself. Even granting biblical underpinnings to one's ethic, moreover, questions arise concerning the accuracy of the despotic interpretation of human dominion. Although the Hebrew concept of *rada*, translated as "having dominion," is often interpreted to mean human despotism over the nonhuman world, an idea that some early critics (White 1967; McHarg 1969) have characterized as the root cause of today's environmental crisis, more recent thinkers (Barr 1974; Linzey 1976, 1987; McDaniel 1989; Callicott 1993) have proposed a significantly different interpretation. *Rada* can be understood as the idea of human responsibility for and care of a created order that is *good independent of the human presence*. According to this latter interpretation, commonly referred to as stewardship, humans are charged with loving the natural order as much as God did when creating it. Humans, that is, are to be the loving caretakers of an independently good creation. Indeed, according to the stewardship perspective, it is precisely because the natural world and particularly nonhuman animals are good apart from human interests that our duties with regard to these animals emerge as direct duties owed to them rather than indirect duties owed either to other humans or to their creator.

Although this interpretation assigns to all of creation a value independent of human interests, the value of nonhuman animals arguably is especially noteworthy. One might note, first, that these animals were created on the same day—the sixth—as were humans (Gen. 1:24–27); that in the original state of perfection, in Eden, humans did not eat other animals (Gen. 1:29); and that, in God's covenant with Noah after the Flood (Gen. 9:8–12), animals (but not plants) are included. Using these images, one can argue that the choice we face today is *either* to continue to move further away from the sort of relationship with the animals God hoped would prevail when the world was created *or* to make daily efforts to recapture that relationship— to journey back to Eden, as it were. Given this latter reading, the practical consequences of a stewardship interpretation of dominion would depart significantly from those favored by the status-quo position, just as the goals one would hope to achieve would differ from those advanced by reformists. If our righteous relationship with the other animals in our capacities as their caretakers and protectors is one of nonutilization (they are not to be eaten, not to be worn, etc.), the stewardship interpretation of human dominion seems to support an abolitionist ideal.

However these matters are to be settled, the biblical grounding of morality characteristic of both despotism and stewardship places these moral perspectives outside the mainstream of normative ethical theory, at least from the Enlightenment forward, where rigorous, imaginative attempts have been made to ground ethics independently of belief in God and the moral authority of the Bible. One such attempt is contractarianism.

Contractarianism

Among the most influential nontheological political and moral theories, contractarianism has a legacy that reaches at least as far back as Thomas Hobbes (1968 [1651]) and includes such notable contemporary philosophers as John Rawls (1971) and Jan Narveson (1989). Like other theorists united by a common outlook, contractarians often disagree on many of the most fundamental points. It will not be possible to do justice to the rich fabric of disagreement that characterizes proponents of this or the other theories under review.

As its name suggests, contractarianism conceives of morality as a kind of contract into which people (the "contractors") voluntarily enter. For contractarians, morality emerges as a set of mutually agreed on and enforceable constraints on human freedom, constraints that each contractor rationally believes to be in his or her own self-interest. According to contractarian theory, then, nothing is by its very nature morally right or wrong, just or unjust; rather, acts or institutions become right or wrong, just or unjust, as a result of the agreements reached by rational, self-interested contractors. In this sense, all morality is conventional; none, natural. Morality is created, not discovered, by human beings.

Both the self-interest that motivates and the rationality that guides the contractors are significant. We are not to imagine that, in their deliberations about acceptable limits on their freedom, contractors are motivated by a natural sympathy for the misfortune of others or that they are willing altruistically to accept personal loss so that others might gain. Each contractor is exclusively motivated by his or her self-interest. Moreover, the relevant conception of individual self-interest is neither whimsical nor uninformed. Each contractor asks the same basic question: From the point of view of what is best for me, rationally considered, what limitations on my freedom would I be willing to accept? Morality, understood as rational, enforceable constraints on human freedom, arises when all the contractors jointly agree on the same constraints, again, not out of sympathy for others or because of altruistic motivations but because each judges the outcome to be in his or her personal self-interest.

Two forms of contractarianism may be distinguished. The first permits the contractors to enter into their contractual deliberations knowing who they are and what they want out of life, given their individual interests, talents, and hopes. This is the form of contractarianism favored by Hobbes and Narveson, for example. The second, favored by Rawls, requires the contractors to imagine that they lack such detailed knowledge of their individual psychology and circumstances and instead deliberate about the terms of the contract from behind what Rawls calls "a veil of ignorance." I will explain momentarily why Rawls would have recourse to this imaginative point of view. First, however, we should consider what Hobbesian contractarianism implies for the treatment of nonhuman animals.

Judged on the basis of the interests of these animals themselves, the implications are not particularly salutary. Given their inability to express these interests and to negotiate with others, nonhuman animals obviously are not to be counted among the potential contractors. Even though it is true that some things are in the interests of, say, pigs and wolves, the idea that these animals themselves can have an informed understanding of their rational self-interests has no clear meaning. Not surprisingly, therefore, Hobbesian contractarianism protects these animals only insofar as human contractors happen to have certain interests in them.

Narveson (1989a), for one, cheerfully indicates that this interest need not be very much. Since many contractors have special places in their hearts for companion animals ("pets"), these animals should be treated reasonably well not because they themselves are entitled to such treatment but because we should not upset their human friends gratuitously. In the case of most other nonhuman animals, however, including those slaughtered for food or used in research, Narveson finds no good reason to cease and desist. Clearly, then, given Hobbesian contractarianism, all our duties with respect to other animals are indirect duties owed to those human beings who help forge the contract. Just as clearly, considered from a political perspective, one finds little within this version of contractarianism that could mount an abolitionist or a far-reaching reformist approach to the treatment of other animals; what one finds instead is a theory well disposed to the status quo while remaining open to modest reforms.

Critics of Hobbesian contractarianism have raised a variety of objections (Regan 1983). One concerns the possibility of arbitrary discrimination between people—for example, discrimination based on race. If we imagine that a large majority of potential contractors (say, 95 percent) are white and the remainder are black, then it is not obviously irrational for those who constitute the majority to exclude members of the minority from negotiating the contract; perhaps the majority might even agree to keep the minority in bondage, as chattel slaves, the better to advance the rational self-interests of those individuals in the majority. That such an arrangement would be unjust seems too obvious to need a supporting argument, and for Hobbesian contractarianism, there's the rub. Since the just and unjust are created through the agreements reached by the contractors, this form of contractarianism provides no theoretical grounding for the evident injustice involved in excluding the minority from participating. That is, the theory not only fails to illuminate why such discrimination is unjust; it also deprives us of the means even to raise this objection. If a moral theory is so fundamentally flawed with regard to the treatment of human beings of different skin pigmentation, it is unclear how it can be any nearer the truth with regard to the treatment of nonhuman beings of different species.

Rawls's proposed veil of ignorance, mentioned earlier, can be interpreted as his attempt to preserve the spirit of Hobbesian contractarianism while departing importantly from the letter. Rawls invites would-be contractors to imagine themselves in what he calls the "original position," in which, because they deliberate from behind the veil of ignorance, they do not know when or where they will be born or whether they will be rich or poor, of exceptional intelligence or below average, male or female, Caucasian or non-Caucasian. All the contractors must then ask what limits on human freedom they will accept in the face of such profound ignorance.

The full scope of Rawls's answer need not concern us. Only two points are of particular importance here. The first concerns how Rawlsian contractarianism is preferable to Hobbesian contractarianism because of the way it addresses the issue of discrimination based on race. As already noted, Hobbesian contractors can have a self-interested reason for accepting such discrimination if they know they belong to a racial majority. Rawlsian contractors, in contrast, lack such a reason since, for all they know, *they* might turn out to be among the minority. In this respect Rawlsian contractarianism seems to constitute a notable improvement over Hobbesian contractarianism.

Despite its apparent strengths in response to issues involving arbitrary discrimination, Rawls's account of the moral status of nonhuman animals seems to fail to live up to its own standards (VanDeVeer 1979). While the imaginary contractors behind the veil of ignorance are denied detailed knowledge about their individual interests and circumstances, and thus do not know whether, say, they will be male or female, or black or white, Rawls does permit them to know that they will be born as human beings. To allow knowledge of this detail, however, seems to prejudice the case against nonhuman animals from the start. Granted, rational, self-interested contractors making choices from behind the veil of ignorance will negotiate direct duties to human beings and indirect ones to nonhumans *if they know they will be born human.* But this shows only that contractors will discriminate against nonhuman animals when they are provided with an arbitrary reason for doing so. In short, neither Hobbesian nor Rawlsian contractarianism seems to offer a reasonable basis on which to ground the only sorts of duty each recognizes in the case of nonhuman animals—namely, indirect duties.

Kantianism

A final example of an indirect duty view is provided by the great Prussian philosopher Immanuel Kant. In some respects Kant's moral philosophy regarding the treatment of nonhuman animals is an amalgam of Aristotle's and, stripped of its appeals to God, Aquinas's. In concert with both, Kant emphasizes rationality as the defining characteristic of being human, and echoing St. Thomas, he objects to cruelty to animals because of the deleterious effect this has on the treatment of humans. "He who is cruel to animals," Kant writes, "becomes hard also in his dealings with men," whereas "tender feelings towards dumb animals develop humane feelings towards mankind" (Kant 1976:123).

Despite these historical echoes, Kant's moral philosophy is in many ways highly original. Of particular note is Kant's thesis that humanity exists as "end in itself." Kant does not attempt to prove this thesis by appeal to some more basic principle; rather, it is set forth as a postulate in his system. In this capacity it serves the function of placing humans and other rational, autonomous beings in a unique moral category, one that distinguishes them, as "persons," from everything else that exists. Indeed, like Aristotle and Aquinas before him, Kant views the rest of the natural order as existing to serve human interests. In particular, animals, in his words, exist "merely as a means to an end. That end is man" (Kant 1976:123). Thus, whereas on Kant's view we are morally free to use other animals as we wish, subject only to the injunction to avoid cruelty, we are not morally free to treat human beings in a comparable fashion. Because humans exist as ends in themselves, we are never to treat them merely as means, Kant argues, which is what we would be doing if we treated them as we treat other animals (for example, if we raised humans as a food source). An abolitionist, a radical reformist, Kant is not. Provided only that we are not cruel in our treatment of nonhuman animals, we do nothing wrong when we treat them as we do.

A common objection urged against Kant's position is the argument from marginal cases (Narveson 1977; Regan 1983). All humans, Kant implies, exist as ends in themselves. To restrict this supreme moral value to humans only among terrestrial creatures is not arbitrary, Kant believes, because unlike the other animals, humans are unique in being rational and autonomous. However, not all humans are rational and autonomous. Humans who are mentally enfeebled and deranged, for example, lack these capacities. Are these humans nevertheless ends in themselves? If Kant's answer is affirmative, then the presence of rationality and autonomy does not ground this supreme moral value; if Kant's answer is negative, then these "marginal" human beings do not exist as ends in themselves, in which case it would seem that these humans, no less than other animals, may be treated as mere means. Because presumably Kant would have seen this latter consequence to be morally grotesque, it seems fair to assume that he would have wanted to avoid it; but he could do so, it seems, only by accepting the view that individuals who are neither rational nor autonomous nevertheless exist as ends in themselves, a view that undermines his confident assertion that nonhuman animals, deficient in reason and autonomy as he claims they are, exist "merely as means to an end," the end being "man."

Utilitarianism

The pioneering work of the nineteenth-century utilitarians Jeremy Bentham (1976) and John Stuart Mill (1976) represent a significant departure from the enduring Aristotelian legacy we find in Kant's moral theory. Bentham, referring to nonhuman animals, writes, "The question is not, Can they *reason*? nor, Can they *talk*? but, Can they *suffer*?" (1976:130). The possession of *sentience* (the capacity to experience pleasure and pain), not the possession of rationality, autonomy, or linguistic competence, entitles any individual to direct moral consideration; because nonhuman animals have this capacity, Bentham and Mill affirm our direct duty not to cause them needless suffering. *We owe it to these animals themselves*, not those humans who might be affected by what we do, to consider their pleasures and pains and, having done so, to ensure that we never make them suffer without good reason.

Both Bentham and Mill give a utilitarian interpretation of the form such a reason might take. Roughly speaking, utilitarianism is the view that our duty is to perform the act that will bring about the best consequences for all those affected by the outcome. For value hedonists such as Bentham and Mill, who recognize only one intrinsic good (pleasure) and only one intrinsic evil (pain), the best consequences will be those that include the greatest possible balance of pleasure over pain. A good reason for permitting animal suffering, then, is that such suffering is a necessary price to pay in bringing about the best consequences, all considered. Individual utilitarians advocate reform, abolition, or the status quo depending on the extent to which they judge animal suffering to be necessary. Bentham opposes hunting, fishing, and animal baiting for sport, for example, and Mill's name is to be found among those of the earliest contributors to England's Royal Society for the Prevention of Cruelty to Animals. Nevertheless, neither Bentham nor Mill aligns himself with the cause of antivivisection, and both were lifelong meat eaters. So reformers they are, but abolitionists they are not. Even so, given the broader social context in which they lived, many of their contemporaries viewed them as radicals, if not extremists.

The degree to which utilitarians can differ over important practical matters is illustrated in our time by Peter Singer and R. G. Frey. Singer is justly famous for his seminal book *Animal Liberation* (1975), and Frey has authored two books and many essays devoted to the issues under review. Although agreeing on some of the most fundamental points in ethical theory, the two philosophers disagree on many of the most important consequences each believes follow from the application of utilitarianism, including the acceptable treatment of nonhuman animals. For example, in *Animal Liberation* Singer advocates vegetarianism on moral grounds; Frey disagrees, appealing to the same grounds in *Rights, Killing, and Suffering: Moral Vegetarianism and Applied Eth-*

ics (1983). It will be useful to explain how such profound disagreements can arise between partisans of the same moral philosophy.

By its very nature, utilitarianism is a forward-looking moral theory. The consequences of our actions, and the consequences alone, determine the morality of what we do. As such, utilitarians will reach opposing judgments about an act's rightness or wrongness if they have opposing views of its consequences. In the case of vegetarianism in particular, utilitarians such as Singer believe that, taking everyone's interests into account and counting equal interests equally, the consequences that flow from abstaining from animal flesh will be better than those resulting from its consumption; Frey, however, believes that the benefits of a vegetarian diet are not so great that they oblige us to become vegetarians. Thus, factual disagreements over future consequences underlie the type of moral disagreement that separates Singer and Frey on the particular issue of vegetarianism.

Some critics of utilitarianism (Clark 1977) argue that the apparently irresolvable impasse created by Singer's and Frey's application of utilitarian theory to the particular case of vegetarianism illustrates a major weakness in the theory in general. Because much—indeed, everything—depends on our limited ability to know what will happen in the future, these critics maintain that utilitarianism reduces moral judgment to guesswork about possible results.

Despite this problem, utilitarianism may seem to be a congenial theory for those who utilize nonhuman animals in animal-model research. The most common justification of such research consists in appealing to the improvements in human health and longevity to which this research allegedly has led, and while researchers may recognize the need to look for alternatives to the animal model, lest these animals be used unnecessarily, it seems clear that the moral justification they offer is utilitarian. (For dissenting voices regarding the human benefits of such research from the perspective of the history of medicine, see McKinlay and McKinlay 1977; for epistemological concerns, see LaFollette and Shanks 1992). Part of the enduring greatness of *Animal Liberation* lies in Singer's relentless documentation showing how much of this research prima facie fails to meet the utilitarian standard favored by researchers themselves. No less important is the way Singer exposes a prejudice that he, following Richard Ryder (Ryder 1975), denominates "speciesism" and that he characterizes as "an attitude of bias in favor of the interests of members of one's own species and against those of other species" (Singer 1990:6). Research scientists, Singer believes, frequently offer at best half a utilitarian justification of their work: human interests are considered; those of nonhuman animals are not. To be consistent, the interests of both must be counted, and counted equitably. It is Singer's considered judgment that few researchers are consistent in this regard.

Frey (1980), too, examines the lack of moral consistency among researchers. Given any reasonable view about the richness and variety of psychological life, it is unquestionably true, Frey believes, that the psychological life of a nonhuman primate, or even of a cat or a dog, is richer and more varied than the psychological life of some human beings (for example, a child born with only the stem of the brain). Thus, if the moral defense of animal-model research is supposed to lie in the good results allegedly produced by using these animals, then a similar defense for utilizing marginal humans is at hand. To be consistent in their utilitarianism, therefore, Frey believes that researchers should be willing to conduct their studies on marginal humans. Researchers are unlikely to welcome Frey's finding. For his part, Frey is untroubled, insisting that researchers cannot have it both ways, using utilitarian modes of thinking when they believe it justifies their practice of using other-than-human animals in their studies, only to discard utilitarianism when its implications for the selection of marginal humans as research subjects are made manifest.

Whatever form utilitarianism takes, one of the principal objections its advocates face centers on questions of justice (Lyons 1965). What limits, if any, can utilitarianism recognize on the methods by which future good is to be obtained? The theory seems to imply that good ends justify whatever means are necessary to achieve them, including means that are flagrantly unjust. Classic examples include situations in which the judicial execution of the innocent is sanctioned on the grounds that others will be deterred from committing similar offenses. Here, critics concede, good consequences are brought into being, but the means used to secure them are reprehensible because unjust.

Utilitarians have replies to this and similar lines of criticism that go beyond the scope of the present essay (Brandt 1979). Suffice it to say that many nonutilitarians dissociate themselves from utilitarianism because they believe that the principle of respect for an individual's rights should not be compromised in the name of achieving some greater good for others. Not surprisingly, perhaps, a position of this kind, one that prohibits the use of nonhuman animals in the name of advancing the general human welfare, has been advanced (Regan 1983). Although not the only possible theory of animal rights (see, for example, Rollin 1981, 1989), this particular theory (the "rights view") can be seen as an attempt to blend certain features of utilitarianism and Kant's theory.

The Rights View

Kant, it will be recalled, recognizes only indirect duties to nonhuman animals; for example, we should not treat them cruelly not because doing so wrongs them but because it can lead us to be cruel to one another. In contrast, utilitarians from Bentham to Singer recognize direct duties to nonhuman animals; they believe that there are certain things we owe to these animals themselves, apart from how humans will be affected. On this divisive issue the rights view sides with utilitarians against Kantians: nonhuman animals are of direct moral significance; we have direct duties in their case.

In a second respect, however, the rights view sides with Kantians against utilitarians. Utilitarians believe that duty is determined by the comparative value of consequences: the right thing to do is whatever causes the best results. Kant and his followers take a decidedly different view: what is right depends not on the value of consequences but on the appropriate, respectful treatment of the individual—in particular, their treatment as ends, not merely means. In this regard the rights view is cut from Kantian, not utilitarian, cloth. What is right depends not on the value of consequences but on the appropriate, respectful treatment of the individual, including individual nonhuman animals. Thus, the fundamental principle of the rights view (the respect principle) is Kantian in spirit: we are to treat individuals who exist as ends in themselves (those who have inherent value) always as ends, never merely as means.

One problem the rights view faces concerns determining which nonhuman animals possess value of this kind. Like many other line-drawing issues ("Exactly how tall do you have to be to be tall?" or "Exactly how old do you have to be to be old?"), this one has no precise resolution, in part because the criterion for drawing the line is itself imprecise. The criterion the rights view proposes (Regan 1983:243–48) is that of being the *subject of a life*, a criterion that specifies a set of psychological capacities (for example, the capacities to desire, remember, act intentionally, and feel emotions) as jointly sufficient for such value. At least some nonhuman animals (for example, mammalian animals and birds) arguably possess these capacities; they are thus subjects of a life and, given the rights view, to be treated as ends in themselves (for criticism, see Frey 1980).

For obvious reasons, such a view has massive political, social, and moral implications. From an animal rights perspective, duty requires the abolition of human exploitation of these animals, whether on the farm, at the lab, or in the wild, not merely the reform of these practices, and certainly not approval of the status quo.

Line-drawing issues to one side, the rights view faces daunting challenges from other quarters. One concerns the idea of inherent value. Some critics (Sapontzis 1987) allege that the idea is "mystifying," meaning that it lacks any clear meaning. Advocates of animal rights reply that the notion of inherent value is no less "mystifying" than Kant's idea of end in itself. As applied to human beings, Kant's idea of an end in itself is an attempt to articulate the cherished belief that the value or worth of a human being is not reducible to instrumental value—not reducible, that is, to a human being's usefulness in forwarding the interests or purposes of other human beings. On Kant's view, neither John nor Jane Doe exists as a mere resource relative to what other people want for themselves, and to treat the Does as if their value—their worth or dignity—consists merely in their resource or instrumental value for others is morally wrong. All that the rights view alleges is that the same moral judgment be made in those cases where non-human animals who are subjects of a life are treated in a similar fashion.

Another set of challenges alleges that acting on the philosophy of animal rights would lead to catastrophic consequences, either to human interests in particular or to the community of life in general. Concerning the former challenge, some critics argue that human health and longevity would be seriously harmed if, as the philosophy of animal rights requires, nonhuman animals ceased to be used as models of human disease (Gallistel 1981; Cohen 1986). Several responses seem apposite.

First, given the massive allocation of public money to fund such research, it needs to be asked whether abandoning reliance on the whole animal model really is contrary to the collective best interests of human beings. Some (Sharpe 1988) argue that customary reliance on this well-entrenched scientific methodology retards the development of alternative methodologies that would be more useful in understanding and curing major human diseases; in addition, these critics insist that humans would benefit more if the dominant focus of biomedical research were shifted away from curing disease and toward preventing it, a goal that they claim would be more efficiently advanced by methodologies other than the use of the whole animal model.

Second, recall one of the fundamental objections raised against utilitarianism: just as one does not justify violating a human being's rights because doing so will benefit others, so one does not justify violating the rights of nonhuman animals on similar grounds. More generally, some gains may be ill gotten, and they are ill gotten if the price of obtaining them involves the violation of another's rights. Thus, even if humans do stand to lose some benefits if animal-model research is abandoned, this by itself does not constitute a telling moral objection to the abolitionist implications of the philosophy of animal rights, assuming that these animals, like humans, have the right to be treated as ends in themselves.

Concerning the second line of criticism—the one that alleges that acting on the philosophy of animal rights would have catastrophic implications for the community of life in general—the principal objection may be summarized as follows. Predatory animals obviously live off the death and flesh of their prey. Because the rights view accords prey animals the right to be treated with respect, some critics (Callicott 1980; Sagoff 1984) claim it to imply that we should intervene to stop predatory animals in their natural depredations. If we were to do this, however, then there would be no check on the ratio of predators to prey; instead, the population of prey animals would explode, and this would irreparably damage the balance and sustainability of life forms within the larger life community.

Advocates of the philosophy of animal rights have a number of possible replies to the predation problem (Sapontzis 1987:229–48), the principal one being the following. Situations can and do arise where it is right to come to the assistance of another, whether the potential victim is a human or a nonhuman animal. In these situations, however, the potential victim is not only at risk of serious injury but also less than capable of mounting a defense. For example, an elderly woman who is attacked by a psychotic killer or a puppy who is being tormented by children merits our intervention. The predator-prey relationship seems to bear little resemblance to such cases. Most prey animals, most of the time, are perfectly capable of eluding their predators without anyone's assistance. Thus it seems to be human arrogance, not informed responsibility, that leads humans to believe that the rights of wild animals obligate us to "police" nature. From an animal rights perspective, we have no general duty to intervene in predator-prey relations; that being so, the catastrophic environmental costs alleged to follow from acting on the rights view seem to be more fiction than fact.

Deep Ecology

Despite the significant differences separating the philosophy of animal rights and other, more traditional moral theories, such as Kant's, there are also important similarities. For example, like Kant's theory, the philosophy of animal rights recognizes the noninstrumental value of the individual. Moreover, like both Kant's theory and utilitarianism, animal rights philosophy articulates an abstract, universal, and impartial fundamental moral principle— abstract because the respect principle enjoins us to treat others with respect without regard to the special circumstances of time, or place, or circumstance; universal because the respect principle applies to everyone capable of making moral decisions; and impartial because this principle does not favor some individuals (for example, family members or companion animals) over others. Some contemporary moral philosophers find this approach to ethics archaic; among these critics some of those who classify themselves as deep ecologists (Devall and Sessions 1985) command a growing audience. (For a more systematic and in some ways different version of deep ecology, see Naess 1989. For importantly different approaches to environmental ethics, see Taylor 1986; Rolston 1988; Callicott 1989.)

Both traditional moral theories and the philosophy of animal rights are doubly to be faulted, according to Devall and Sessions, first, because these moral outlooks offer an overly intellectualized account of the moral life, and second, because they perpetuate the myth of the moral preeminence of the individual. Concerning the latter charge, Devall and Sessions argue that the concept of the isolated, atomistic individual, which arises out of the anthropocentric traditions of Western philosophy, is false to the facts of all life's embeddedness in the larger life community. People are not independent bits of mind existing by themselves; they are enmeshed in networks of relationships that bind them both to their evolutionary past and to their ecological present. Expressed another way, humans do not stand "above" or "apart from" nature; they stand "within" nature. Moreover, the natural world does not exist "for us," as a storehouse of renewable human resources (a view that is symptomatic of a "shallow" view of humanity's relationship to nature); we are inseparable from the natural environment (a view that indicates a "deeper" understanding of what it means to be human). Thus, it is not just that the concept of the isolated individual existing outside the natural order is illusory; what is worse, its acceptance has done and continues to do incalculable damage to those who seek self-understanding. As long as we carry out this quest with a fundamentally flawed preconception of our place in the larger scheme of things, the more we search, the less we will understand.

As for the charge that traditional moral theories overintellectualize the moral life, Devall and Sessions argue that the moral life should be viewed as primarily experiential, not inferential, a life characterized by our coming to experience certain values in the concrete particularities of day-to-day life rather than by apprehending abstract, universal, impartial moral principles by means of our rational powers. Among those values to be found in the concrete particularities of day-to-day life, some involve other animals, and although deep ecologists have not written extensively on some of the most pressing practical issues, the general disdain these thinkers display toward reductionist science and industrial societies' technological domination of the natural world suggests that they would be at least strong reformists regarding such practices as factory farming and animal-model research. In the case of sport and recreational hunting, however, Devall and Sessions not only find nothing wrong with the practice; they applaud it. In pursuit of their prey, hunters tap into natural means whereby, through the act of killing, they can obtain greater self-understanding. Devall and Sessions thus seem to understand our duties with respect to animals as indirect duties limited by the overarching quest for self-knowledge. Therefore, although we can count on deep ecologists such as Sessions and Devall to add their voices to those of reformists and abolitionists in some cases, they emerge as defenders of the status quo in others.

Ecofeminism

Ecofeminists join advocates of the rights view among those contemporary moral philosophers who differ significantly with deep ecologists. Like other "isms," ecofeminism is not a monolithic position (Adams 1990; Diamond and Orenstein 1990; Warren 1990; Gaard 1993); instead, it represents a number of defining tendencies, including in particular a principled stance that puts its advocates on the side of those who historically have been victims of oppression. For obvious reasons, women are pictured as among the oppressed, but the scope of ecofeminism's concern is not limited to women by any means. Ecofeminists maintain that the same ideology that sanctions oppression based on gender also sanctions oppression based on race, class, and physical abilities, among other things. Moreover, they believe that this same ideology sanctions the oppression of nature in general and of nonhuman animals in particular.

In a number of fundamental ways, ecofeminism's diagnosis of the ideology of oppression resembles deep ecology's diagnosis of the deficiencies of traditional moral theory. As does deep ecology, ecofeminism challenges the myth of the isolated individual existing apart from the world and instead affirms the interconnectedness of all life. Moreover, no less than deep ecologists, ecofeminists abjure the overintellectualization of the moral life characteristic of traditional moral theories, with their abstract, universal, and impartial fundamental principles. But whereas deep ecologists locate the fundamental cause of moral theory's misstep in anthropocentrism (humancenteredness), ecofeminists argue that its real cause is androcentrism (malecenteredness).

Nowhere is this difference clearer than in the case of sport or recreational hunting. Devall and Sessions celebrate the value of this practice as a means of bonding ever closer with the natural world, of discovering "self in Self"; ecofeminists, by contrast, detect in the hunt the vestiges of patriarchy—the male's need to dominate and subdue (Kheel 1991). More fundamentally, there is the lingering suspicion that deep ecologists continue to view the value of the natural world instrumentally, as a means to greater self-awareness and self-knowledge. In this respect, and despite appearances to the contrary, deep ecology does not represent a "paradigm shift" away from the anthropocentric worldview it aspires to replace.

Ecofeminists believe they offer a deeper account of the moral life than do deep ecologists, one that goes to the very foundations of Western moral theorizing. The idea of "the rights of the individual" is diagnosed as a symptom of patriarchal thought, rooted as it is in the (male) myth of the isolated individual. A moral paradigm shift occurs when, instead of asserting rights, we freely and lovingly choose to take care of and assume responsibility for victims of oppression, both within and beyond the extended human family, other animals included. Writing for the growing number of ecofeminists, Josephine Donovan states that

> natural rights and utilitarianism present impressive and useful arguments for the ethical treatment of animals. Yet, it is also possible—indeed, necessary—to ground that ethic in an emotional and spiritual conversation with nonhuman life forms. Out of a woman's relational culture of caring and attentive love therefore emerges the basis for a feminist ethic for the treatment of animals. We should not kill, eat, torture, and exploit animals because they do not want to be so treated, and we know that. If we listen, we can hear them. (1993:185)

Thus, whereas the grounds for practical action offered by ecofeminists differ fundamentally from those favored by the rights view, and despite the foundational gulf that separates these two outlooks, both arguably share the same abolitionist practical implications.

Conclusion

The "animal rights debate," broadly conceived, is more than a contest of wills representing professional, economic, and ethical concerns; it is also a divisive, enduring topic in normative ethical theory (Vance 1992). Until comparatively recently, it is true, discussions of the moral status of nonhuman animals had all but disappeared from the work of moral philosophers. (For a historical overview, see Ryder 1989.) Beginning in the 1970s, however, we have witnessed an unprecedented outpouring of philosophical and theological interest in exploring the moral ties that bind humans to other animals (see Godlovitch, Godlovitch, and Harris 1972; Singer 1975; Linzey 1976; Clark 1977), and there is every indication that this interest will intensify in the coming decades. The moral theories of philosophers are not the stuff of politics; still, the contributions philosophers make can help shape the political debate by clarifying the major theoretical options available to an informed public.

Principal among these options are those that have been canvassed here: perfectionism, despotism and stewardship, contractarianism, Kantianism, utilitarianism, the rights view, deep ecology, and ecofeminism. Doubtless other options will evolve as the discussion continues (Garner 1994). Among these current options, two in particular—utilitarianism and the rights view—have offered the most systematic accounts of those duties owed directly to nonhuman animals, and it will be instructive, before concluding, to highlight some of the important practical differences that flow from these competing philosophies.

Because utilitarianism is committed to reducing the total amount of suffering in the world, its proponents must be prepared to recognize the moral legitimacy of some research on nonhuman animals. Even Peter Singer (1993), contemporary utilitarianism's most forceful critic of such research, has conceded this possibility. Moreover, utilitarians must be similarly well disposed to the activities of institutional animal care and use committees (Singer himself has served as a member of such a committee), provided that these committees conscientiously work to eliminate unnecessary animal suffering. Legislative attempts to improve the wellbeing of animals, whether in laboratories or on the farm, also find support among utilitarians. Viewed in these respects, utilitarianism offers a philosophical basis for those who would reform the ways in which nonhuman animals are utilized by humans; what it does not offer is a categorical condemnation of this utilization. It is for this reason that utilitarianism is congenial to those individuals and groups working to advance animal welfare—that is, those who accept the morality of human utilization of nonhuman animals in principle but who seek to improve it in practice by making it more humane.

The rights view takes a different view of such matters (Francione and Regan 1992). This philosophy is opposed to human utilization of nonhuman animals in principle and seeks to end it in practice. Its practical implications are abolitionist, not reformist. Because those nonhuman animals who exist as ends in themselves are never to be treated merely as means, it is wrong to experiment on them in the name of advancing the wellbeing of others. Moreover, to the extent that institutional animal care and use committees and reformist legislation help to perpetuate social acceptance of human exploitation of these animals, whether on the farm or in the laboratory, advocates of the rights view will—or, to be consistent, should—withhold their support. What animal rights advocates *can* consistently support are incremental steps that put an end to certain practices within the larger context of animal exploitation—for example, legislation that would prohibit the use of nonhuman animals in cosmetic testing and in drug addiction experiments and the creation of policies that end compulsory vivisection and dissection in the classroom (Francione and Charlton 1992). When, as can often happen, utilitarians deem such practices unjustified because they cause gratuitous animal suffering, these two conflicting normative ethical philosophies—utilitarianism and the rights view—can speak with one voice. When this happens, their potential political power is greater than the sum of its parts.

No one can predict which of the tendencies examined in the preceding—reform, abolition, or the status quo—will prevail in the coming years. Some positions (for example, the rights view and ecofeminism) call for fundamental social change; others (for example, Aristotelian perfectionism and Kant's view) call for much less. To the extent that people act because of their beliefs, the future of humans' behavior toward other animals depends on what we humans believe them to be and how we think they should be treated. Because what we should do in practice depends on understanding what we ought to do in principle, our ability to give an appropriate response to the practical issues constituting the animal rights debate, broadly conceived—from asking whether we ought to be vegetarians to deciding whether we should encourage sport or recreational hunting—depends on our ability to make an informed, rational choice among normative ethical theories. In this respect, although a fair consideration of such theories may not be the end-all, it can make some claim to being at least part of the begin-all of a commitment to seek understanding and truth in these troubled waters.

Works Cited

Adams, Carol. 1990. *The Sexual Politics of Meat: A Feminist-Vegetarian Critical Theory*. New York: Continuum.

Aquinas, St. Thomas. 1976. "On Killing Living Things and the Duty to Irrational Creatures." In *Animal Rights and Human Obligations*, ed. Tom Regan and Peter Singer, 119. Englewood Cliffs, N.J.: Prentice-Hall; repr. in idem, *Animal Rights and Human Obligations*, 2d ed., 11. Englewood Cliffs, N.J.: Prentice-Hall, 1989.

Aristotle. 1976. "Animals and Slavery." In *Animal Rights and Human Obligations*, ed. Tom Regan and Peter Singer, 109–10. Englewood Cliffs, N.J.: Prentice-Hall; repr. in idem, *Animal Rights and Human Obligations*, 2d ed., 4–5. Englewood Cliffs, N.J.: Prentice-Hall, 1989.

Barr, James. 1974. "Man and Nature: The Ecological Controversy over the Old Testament." In *Ecology and Religion in History*, ed. D. Springs and E. Springs, 58–72. New York: Harper and Row/Torchbooks.

Bentham, Jeremy. 1976. "A Utilitarian View." In *Animal Rights and Human Obligations*, ed. Tom Regan and Peter Singer, 129–30. Englewood Cliffs, N.J.: Prentice-Hall; repr. in idem, *Animal Rights and Human Obligations*, 2d ed., 25–26. Englewood Cliffs, N.J.: Prentice-Hall, 1989.

Brandt, R. B. 1979. *A Theory of the Good and the Right*. Oxford: Clarendon.

Callicott, J. Baird. 1980. "Animal Liberation: A Triangular Affair," *Environmental Ethics* 2, no. 4:311–28; repr. in J. Baird Callicott, *In Defense of the Land Ethic*, 15–38. Albany, N.Y: SUNY Press, 1989.

———. 1989. *In Defense of the Land Ethic*, 15–38. Albany, N.Y.: SUNY Press.

———. 1993. "The Search for an Environmental Ethic." In *Matters of Life and Death: New Introductory Essays in Moral Philosophy*, ed. Tom Regan, 3d ed., 322–82. New York: McGraw-Hill.

Clark, Stephen S. L. 1977. *The Moral Status of Animals*. Oxford: Clarendon.

Cohen, Carl. 1986. "The Case for the Use of Animals in Biomedical Research." *New England Journal of Medicine* 315, no. 14 (Oct. 2): 865–70.

Descartes, Rene. 1976. "Animals Are Machines." In *Animal Rights and Human Obligations*, ed. Tom Regan and Peter Singer, 60–66. Englewood Cliffs, N.J.: Prentice-Hall; repr. in idem, *Animal Rights and Human Obligations*, 2d ed., 13–19. Englewood Cliffs, N.J.: Prentice-Hall, 1989.

Devall, Bill, and George Sessions. 1985. *Deep Ecology: Living as if Nature Mattered*. Salt Lake City, Utah: Peregrine Smith Books.

Diamond, Irene, and Gloria Orenstein, eds. 1990. *Reweaving the World: The Emergence of Ecofeminism*. San Francisco: Sierra Club Books.

Donovon, Josephine. 1993. "Animal Rights and Feminist Theory." In *Ecofeminism: Women, Animals, Nature*, ed. Greta Gaard, 167–94. Philadelphia: Temple University Press.

Francione, Gary, and Anna Charlton. 1992. *Vivisection and Dissection in the Classroom: A Guide to Conscientious Objection.* Jenkintown, Pa.: American Anti-Vivisection Society.

Francione, Gary, and Tom Regan. 1992. "A Movement's Means Create Its Ends." *The Animals' Agenda,* January–February, pp. 40–43.

Frey, R. G. 1980. *Interests and Rights: The Case against Animals.* Oxford: Clarendon.

———. 1983. *Rights, Killing, and Suffering: Moral Vegetarianism and Applied Ethics.* Oxford: Clarendon.

Gaard, Greta, ed. 1993. *Ecofeminism: Women, Animals, Nature.* Philadelphia: Temple University Press.

Garner, Richard. 1994. *Beyond Morality.* Philadelphia: Temple University Press.

Godlovitch, R., S. Godlovitch, and J. Harris, eds. 1972. *Animals, Men, and Morals.* New York: Taplinger.

Hobbes, Thomas. 1968 [1651]. *Leviathan.* Ed. C. P. Macpherson. Harmondsworth, U.K.: Penguin.

Kant, Immanuel. 1976. "Duties to Animals." In *Animal Rights and Human Obligations,* ed. Tom Regan and Peter Singer, 123. Englewood Cliffs, N.J.: Prentice-Hall; repr. in idem, *Animal Rights and Human Obligations,* 2d ed., 24. Englewood Cliffs, N.J.: Prentice-Hall, 1989.

Kheel, Marti. 1991. "Ecofeminism and Deep Ecology: Reflections on Identity and Difference." *The Trumpeter* 8, no. 1:62–72.

LaFollette, H., and N. Shanks. 1992. "Animal Models in Biomedical Research: Some Epistemological Worries." *Public Affairs Quarterly* 7, no. 2:250–70.

Linzey, Andrew. 1976. *Animal Rights: A Christian Assessment of Man's Treatment of Animals.* Oxford: Clarendon.

———. 1987. *Christianity and the Rights of Animals.* New York: Crossroad.

McDaniel, Jay B. 1989. *Of God and Pelicans: A Theology of Reverence for Life.* Louisville, Ky.: John Knox Press.

McHarg, Ian. 1969. *Design with Nature.* Philadelphia: Falcon.

McKinlay, J. B., and S. McKinlay. 1977. *Health and Society.* London: Milbank.

Mill, John Stuart. 1976. "A Defense of Bentham." In *Animal Rights and Human Obligations,* ed. Tom Regan and Peter Singer, 131–32. Englewood Cliffs, N.J.: Prentice-Hall.

Naess, Arne. 1989. *Ecology, Community, and Lifestyle.* Ed. and trans. David Rothenberg. Cambridge: Cambridge University Press.

Narveson, Jan. 1977. "Animal Rights." *The Canadian Journal of Philosophy* 7, no. 1:161–78.

———. 1989. *The Libertarian Idea.* Philadelphia: Temple University Press.

Rawls, John. 1971. *A Theory of Justice.* Cambridge, Mass.: Harvard University Press.

Regan, Tom. 1983. *The Case for Animal Rights.* Berkeley: University of California Press.

Regan, Tom, and Peter Singer, eds. 1976. *Animal Rights and Human Obligations.* Englewood Cliffs, N.J.: Prentice-Hall.

———, eds. 1989. *Animal Rights and Human Obligations.* 2d ed. Englewood Cliffs, N.J.: Prentice-Hall.

Rollin, Bernard. 1981. *Animal Rights and Human Morality*. Buffalo, N.Y.: Prometheus Books.

———. 1989. *The Unheeded Cry*. New York: Oxford University Press.

Ryder, Richard. 1975. *Victims of Science: The Use of Animals in Science*. London: Davis-Poynter.

———. 1989. *Animal Revolution: Changing Attitudes towards Speciesism*. Oxford: Blackwell.

Sagoff, Mark. 1984. "Animal Liberation and Environmental Ethics: Bad Marriage, Quick Divorce." *Osgood Hall Law Journal* 22, no. 2:303–4.

Sapontzis, Stephen. 1987. *Morals, Reason, and Animals*. Philadelphia: Temple University Press.

Sharpe, Robert. 1988. *The Cruel Deception: The Use of Animals in Research*. London: Thorsons.

Singer, Peter. 1975. *Animal Liberation*. New York: New York Review Books; dist. Random House.

———. 1990. *Animal Liberation*. 2d ed. New York: New York Review Books; dist. Random House.

———. 1993. "Animals and the Value of Life." In *Matters of Life and Death: New Introductory Essays in Moral Philosophy*, ed. Tom Regan, 3d ed., 280–321. New York: Random House.

Taylor, Paul. 1986. *Respect for Nature: A Theory of Environmental Ethics*. Princeton, N.J.: Princeton University Press.

Vance, Richard P. 1992. "An Introduction to the Philosophical Presuppositions of the Animal Liberation/Rights Movement." *Journal of the American Medical Association* 268:1715–19.

VanDeVeer, Donald. 1979. "Of Beasts, Persons, and the Original Position." *The Monist* 62, no. 4:368–77.

Warren, Karen J. 1990. "The Power and Promise of Ecological Feminism." *Environmental Ethics* 12, no. 2:125–46.

White, Lynn, Jr. 1967. "The Historical Roots of Our Ecological Crisis." *Science* 155:1203–7.

White, Robert J. 1990. *Hastings Center Report* 20 (Nov.–Dec.): 43.

2

ANIMAL LIBERATION: WHAT'S IN A NAME?

On two occasions in the recent past, Great Britain's Royal Society for the Prevention of Cruelty to Animals (RSPCA) organized international conferences that addressed animal rights. The first, which focused exclusively on that topic, was held at Trinity College, the University of Cambridge, in 1977; the second, which addressed broader themes ("Animal Welfare and the Environment" was the title chosen by the RSPCA), used the facilities of Christchurch, University of Oxford, in 1990.

The earlier gathering issued a declaration that was signed by the more than one hundred and fifty people in attendance. It reads as follows.

The Rights of Animals
A Declaration Against Speciesism
Inasmuch as we believe that there is ample evidence that many other species are capable of feeling, we condemn totally the infliction of suffering upon our brother animals, and the curtailment of their enjoyment, unless it be necessary for their individual benefit.

We do not accept that a difference in species alone (any more than a difference in race) can justify wanton exploitation or oppression in the name of science or sport, or for food, commercial profit or other human gain.

We believe in the evolutionary and moral kinship of all animals and we declare our belief that all sentient creatures have rights to life, liberty and the quest for happiness.

We call for the protection of these rights.

Obviously the world had not come around to "protecting these rights" by the time of the second RSPCA-sponsored conference; if it had, that second conference would have been superfluous.

Although I have revised it in some respects, "Animal Liberation: What's in a Name?" is essentially the same presentation I made to the 1990 meeting. It therefore may have something of an "insider's" tone, after the fashion of one animal advocate talking with other animal advocates, but its main points are essentially philosophical. The plain fact is that not all descriptions of animal advocacy mean the same thing; how one chooses to describe the cause one advocates, therefore, is not "merely a matter of semantics." Moreover, even when the words chosen "fit" the cause, so to speak, they may lend themselves to different interpretations; that, too, can make more than a semantic difference, something I illustrate by contrasting two different interpretations of the idea of animal liberation, rejecting the one and accepting the other.

"Animal Liberation: What's in a Name?" was originally published in *Animal Welfare and the Environment*, ed. Richard Ryder, 49–61 (London: Duckworth, 1992), and is reproduced by permission of Duckworth Ltd.

Organized efforts to protect other animals are at a historic crossroads. Never before have so many joined in the struggle to significantly improve their lives. The number of people involved and their growing sense of shared values are making a difference in the political process, in the marketplace, in the classroom, and even—on rare occasions—in places of worship. Truly, animal protection efforts are a force to be reckoned with.

This reckoning sometimes takes bitter forms. Especially among those whose professional training, careers, and economic interests involve routine utilization of other animals (e.g., in the course of scientific research or the pursuit of commerce), some animal advocates are being "reckoned with" with a vengeance. Increasing amounts of time, energy, and money are being devoted to animal rights, with a view not to determining the merits of the issues involved but to weakening or destroying the animal rights movement by discrediting its participants. No longer do we confront the old rhetoric of disdainful dismissal, the one that lumped together all animal advocates as "cranks," "lunatics," "freaks," or simple-minded members of an addled army of "little old ladies in tennis shoes"; this old rhetoric is dead—or dying. In its place is a new rhetoric, an incendiary rhetoric, a rhetoric of vitriolic accusation. Today members of the animal rights movement commonly are said to be "fanatics," "extremists," "radicals," or—the most frequently used verbal bomb—"terrorists." Indeed, it is not unusual to find people using the terms *animal rightist* and *terrorist* interchangeably, as if they were synonyms.

But enough of the incendiary rhetoric that has been, and continues to be, the stock-in-trade of some very powerful voices opposing the animal rights movement. My major interest on this occasion is not to defend the movement against false charges but to clarify certain ideas. For while it is important that animal advocates combat the fraudulent descriptions given by others, it is no less important to find words that adequately describe the movement's ideology and aspirations. Animal advocates say they are against cruelty. They stand for animal welfare, animal protection, compassion, human responsibility to other animals, animal liberation, and animal rights. Do all these ways of speaking say the same thing, or are there important differences? These are the main questions I want to explore on this occasion.

Why Anticruelty Is Not Enough

We do well to remember that societal opposition to cruelty to animals, especially opposition that has the force of law, is a comparatively recent development. In America we find legal prohibitions against cruel treatment of animals in the Massachusetts Bay Colony's 1641 Bodies of Liberties, whereas in England we can date legal sanctions against such cruelty to the passage, on June 22, 1822, of the Ill-Treatment of Cattle Act. Sad to say, there are many countries in which no such laws exist, even to this day.

Laws without strong enforcement are words without deeds, and the tragic truth is that courts in both the United States and Britain have displayed a general unwillingness to mete out harsh punishment to those found guilty of cruelty to animals and an even greater reluctance to render guilty verdicts in the first place. This reluctance stems from understandable reasons, as I will attempt to explain.

In no small measure the scarcity of cruelty convictions is due to the concept of cruelty used in Anglo-American law. Historically, to prohibit cruelty to animals has amounted to prohibiting the infliction of *unnecessary* or *unjustified* pain, especially when the pain is *substantial* and the human agent has acted *wantonly* or *maliciously*, and *with intent*. A man who, for the sheer fun of it, intentionally torments and then sets fire to a cat, knowing full well what he is doing, provides a paradigm example of the sort of behavior laws prohibiting cruelty to animals have historically meant to proscribe.

Few would speak in favor of cruelty to animals as thus understood. Nonetheless, this all but universal consensus conceals important differences, especially those that concern *when* cruelty occurs. There are obvious problems here. To establish that someone acted with malicious or wanton intent is notoriously difficult, all the more so when the inflicted pain is caused by someone who is presumed not to have a malicious or wanton character. Certainly this is a presumption society makes in the case of those professionals who use nonhuman animals in their research. People who are familiar with my writings know that I have consistently defended the characters of the majority of researchers against charges of sadism, Nazism, and the like. My guess is that as a group, CPAs (not to mention moral philosophers) probably are less to be trusted than researchers. I do not deny, and sadly am obliged to admit, the real possibility of incidents of wanton, malicious cruelty in the lab, but I assume these to be the exception, not the rule. Even if "animal-model" research (so-called) is wrong, as I believe it is, it does not follow that only evil people do it.

But establishing cruelty is difficult for another reason. To be told that animals are treated cruelly when they are caused *unnecessary* or *unjustified* pain is of little use unless we are told what counts as unnecessary or unjustified pain. Not surprisingly, different people count differently.

A case in point is the use of rodents to determine whether a given substance causes cancer. Anyone who believes that life for the animals used for this purpose is not all that bad is in denial. There *is* a lot of pain. Except for closet Cartesians, we all can agree on this. But is it unnecessary or unjustified pain? Here I think our consensus is likely to unravel for two importantly different reasons.

First, disagreement can arise concerning the necessity of using rodents to achieve an end that is accepted as morally worthwhile. The end in this case, let us agree, is to protect humans against the cancer-causing powers of a large variety of substances. The potential for disagreement arises because some people will view the rodent as a poor or unreliable model for this purpose, while others will take the contrary view. Given the former viewpoint, causing rodents pain in the course of conducting carcinogen tests is unjustified because the research is bad science and thus a poor way to protect human health. Indeed, a steadily growing number of informed toxicologists are advocating this position. When Philip H. Abelson, writing in the September 21, 1990, lead editorial of the prestigious journal *Science*, claims that "the standard carcinogen tests that use rodents are an obsolescent relic of the ignorance of past decades," it seems safe to say that mainstream scientists, not just animal rights advocates, think we can do better.

The second approach to thinking about the justification of pain does not turn on the value of the science. It is a commonplace that unjust means are sometimes employed to achieve worthwhile ends. In human-to-human ethics, examples abound (for example, parents who murder an unwanted child, collect the insurance, and send their favored daughter off to Oxford). A good end (a daughter's education) is achieved by a vile means.

Is it possible that the same might be true in the case of utilizing rodents in carcinogen tests? Well, people's answers differ. Some people think it is wrong to use these animals as a means to the good end in view; others think such use is permissible. The question, in short, is open to (sometimes heated) debate. As such—and whatever the right answer is, assuming there is a right answer—the question should not be begged. To use nonhuman animals in pursuit of a good end, assuming the end is a good one and the science reliable, does not *guarantee* that all is well morally. To establish that it is, we need to establish that it is not wrong to use these animals in pursuit of a good end—that using them for this purpose is justified, even if they are caused considerable pain. As I say, this is something that needs to be established, not glibly assumed. Indeed, failure to address this question—to beg it—is a good indicator that moral thought and vision are lacking.

The upshot is that merely to affirm one's opposition to cruelty is not enough. Before we can sensibly decide whether causing pain to animals is justified and necessary, or unjustified and unnecessary, the morality of both the ends sought and the means used needs to be assessed.

These same observations can be applied to other ways in which animal advocates describe themselves. People who say they stand for animal protection, compassion, or human responsibility toward the other animals speak well and truly as far as these descriptions go. The problem often is determining how far this is. If these descriptions assume that the only moral prohibition we must honor is the one against cruelty, then they assume that it is *sometimes* morally permissible to cause animals pain, even substantial pain. Since the claim that this is permissible proves to be widely disputed, the position that the notions of animal protection, compassion for animals, or human responsibility to other animals are exhausted by the prohibition against cruelty is question begging, if not simply mistaken.

In addition to suffering these defects, merely being against cruelty to animals is not enough for yet another reason. In the end, all that the prohibition against cruelty forbids is that we not unnecessarily or unjustifiably visit evil, in the form of pain, on another animal. What this prohibition therefore fails to address or explain is the obligation to *promote the good* of other animals. Perhaps no one better exemplifies what a commitment to this ideal means than St. Francis of Assisi. Merely not to hurt animals, or to stop others from doing so, is not enough for him. There is another, higher obligation—namely, to be of service to them by promoting their good, something not captured by the prohibition against cruelty.

The Limits of Animal Welfare

Understood in a particular way, I believe this Franciscan insight captures the essence of the ideals affirmed by those who work for animal welfare. To be for animal welfare, as distinct from merely being against animal cruelty, is to believe that we have a duty to improve the quality of animal life by ensuring—as far as this is practicable, when balanced against our other moral obligations and ideals—that other animals receive what is good for them.

The difference between these two views (anticruelty and pro-welfare) can be illustrated by considering debates about the obligation to enrich the lives of animals in laboratories. Because they are committed to promoting the good of animals, animal welfarists seem to have an intelligible basis on which to rest their call for alleviating the boredom many of these animals experience. To do this, after all, is to improve the welfare of these animals—to make their lives better. Those who limit animal protection to the prohibition against cruelty seem to have a less intelligible basis for encouraging adoption of measures that decrease boredom, assuming that being bored is not the same as being in pain.

Although the anticruelty and pro-welfare viewpoints differ in important ways, I believe animal welfarists have the same strong public support as those who oppose cruelty to animals. Moreover, I believe few people will step forward to denounce the idea of animal welfare, as if it is a matter of indifference whether an animal's life is good or bad. Clearly, there is something in the idea of being for animal welfare that every person of goodwill can accept, just as there is something in the ideas of being against cruelty and for human responsibility and animal protection that these same people can uphold. Nevertheless, as was true in the case of the anticruelty position, the pro-welfare stance is not free of serious problems. I will comment on only one.

Even if all informed people could agree concerning what animal welfare is and how well various animals are faring—and these are very large assumptions, to put the point as mildly as possible—the animal welfarist's position would remain controversial because of what it implies may be done to non-human animals. If we ask an animal welfarist to explain this, we can expect something like the following.

The welfare of nonhuman animals is important, but it is not the only thing that is important. Human interests and preferences also are important, frequently more important than the interests and preferences of other animals. For example, researchers have serious professional and humanitarian interests in the utilization of rodents and other animals used in research. These people are and should be supportive of animal welfare. There is no argument here. But being for animal welfare is perfectly consistent with utilizing other animals in pursuit of human preferences and interests.

There is no question that when animals in laboratories are "sacrificed," we shorten their lives. But ending the lives of animals is not contrary to supporting animal welfare. If animals used in research have fared well, all things considered, up to the point when they are utilized, and if they are killed as humanely as possible, then we do nothing wrong when we kill them.

Moreover, it is important to realize that a commitment to animal welfare is consistent with striving to improve the *overall* condition of those individuals who have a welfare, both humans and other animals, even if this means decreasing the welfare of some individuals. Such circumstances often arise, especially in biomedical research. This is regrettable, certainly, and everything should be done to make the lives of these animals as good as practicable. In the end, however, to diminish the welfare of some animals is a price we must be willing to pay for making the world better, for both humans and others.

This sketch of the position under review shows that animal welfarists attempt to serve two demanding moral masters. First, there is the demand that individual animals have lives that fare well, all things considered. This is the demand that leads animal welfarists to call for improved living conditions for animals in laboratories, for example. Second, there is the demand that welfare be improved in general, and it is this demand that leads animal welfarists to permit the death of some animals, sometimes very large numbers of them, and even to permit the agony of some, so that others might benefit.

When viewed in this light, it should not be surprising that the loudest, most powerful voices speaking in the name of animal welfare today are those of individuals who have an interest in perpetuating institutionalized utilization of nonhuman animals. By this I mean that those who identify themselves with the cause of animal welfare increasingly are those who speak for the commercial animal agriculture community and the biomedical community, for example. Witness the formation, in the U.S. Congress, of the Animal Welfare Caucus and the commercial interests the caucus represents. In the United States, it is fair to say, the major commercial interests that utilize nonhuman animals have usurped the idea of animal welfare from the traditional animal welfare societies.

Some of these societies seem to be unhappy and others embarrassed by this turn of events. Certainly they have a damage-control problem on their hands. How can traditional advocates of animal welfare distance themselves from these new champions of the welfare of animals? Will it be said that, for example, primates raised in breeding colonies do not fare well, all things considered? Well, people who stake their opposition to primate breeding programs on this kind of consideration should be prepared for a long, heated debate, with one set of experts declaring that thus-and-so is true, while another set declares that it is not.

Even if the critics are right, however, and the quality of life for these animals can be improved, this will not change the system in any fundamental way. True, more space might be provided, or perhaps better ventilation or a change in diet or exercise opportunities. That is, the system of utilization might be reformed with a view to improving the welfare of the animals being used. Nevertheless, the philosophy of animal welfare by its very nature permits utilizing other animals for human purposes, even if this means (as it always does) that most of these animals will experience pain, frustration, and other harms, and even if it means, as it almost always does, that these animals will have their lives terminated prematurely. This is what I mean by saying that welfare reforms within the system of utilization will not change the system in any fundamental way.

Animal Rights

Advocates of animal rights believe that more than animal welfare–based reforms of the system are needed. When a system is unjust to the core, respect for justice demands abolition. There is, then, a fundamental moral difference between advocates of anticruelty and animal welfare and advocates of animal rights. Although the first two positions are committed to the view that we are sometimes justified in causing nonhuman animals significant pain in the institutionalized pursuit of valued human interests, animal rightists deny that we are ever justified in doing this. The true objective for which animal advocates should work, according to this view, is not to provide nonhuman animals with larger cages but to empty them. People who describe themselves as advocates of animal rights are therefore expressing a position importantly different from that of people who base their activism on anticruelty or pro-welfare stances. Within the context of biomedical research, to take just one example, animal rightists are abolitionists, not welfare-based reformists.

For reasons I have set forth at length elsewhere (Regan 1983), I believe that the philosophy of animal rights is the right philosophy. The arguments for the "extreme" animal rights position are the best arguments, all things considered—or so I have argued. I do not intend to repeat those arguments here. Instead, I want to say something more about what at first might seem to be a trivial point—namely, how people who share my views should describe themselves. They should not do so simply in terms of being against cruelty or for welfare. That much is clear. But how, then?

Understanding Animal Liberation

People who share my views can and often do describe themselves as being in favor of animal liberation. I believe this is an appropriate description. But I also believe it can be misunderstood.

One possible basis for animal liberation is an egalitarian interpretation of interests (Singer 1975). On this view, the interests of everyone affected by what we do must be taken into account, and equal interests must be counted equally. If only we would do this, we are to suppose, animals would be liberated.

I believe that this understanding of animal liberation is profoundly mistaken. To make this clearer, consider the case of chattel slavery. There is no question that the interests of slaves were often grossly ignored or that when they were considered, they were almost never counted equitably. This much granted, someone might maintain that the fundamental basis for the call to liberate human slaves amounted to the dual demand that their interests (1) not be ignored and (2) be counted equitably.

This is not true. Merely to count the interests of slaves equitably is not equivalent to liberating them. Why? Because slaves can have their interests counted equitably and still remain in bondage. Why? Because there is no guarantee that, once their interests are counted equitably, they should be liberated. Whether they should be liberated will depend on the interests other people have, including the interests of slave owners. Everyone's interests need to be taken into account, and the interests of all need to be weighed equitably. If the results of canvassing interests in this way yield one answer, the slaves should be liberated; if not, then not.

Now this way of thinking about human liberation has got things backward. It is not that, in the face of a system of chattel slavery, we first insist on counting everyone's interests equitably and then see whether slaves should be liberated; rather, we first recognize the moral imperative to liberate them on grounds other than counting equal interests equally. Put another way, after human slaves have been liberated, *then* one might attempt to argue that a fair way to decide between competing social policies is to count everyone's interests and count equal interests equally. But it is profoundly mistaken, I believe, to argue that before we can decide whether human slaves should be liberated, we first need to count everyone's interests, both slaves and slave owners alike, and count equal interests equally. *The interests of those who profit from slavery should play no role whatsoever in deciding whether to abolish the institution that furthers those interests.* The fact that the interests of slaves are not counted equitably by their oppressors proves to be a symptom, not the underlying cause, of the great evil human slaves are made to endure.

This great evil is rooted in systematic injustice. It is the right of slaves to be free, not to be treated as another's property or used as a mere means to another's end; a system of chattel slavery systematically violates these basic moral rights, not the principle that we must count equal interests equally. The very concept of liberation makes sense only if it is viewed against the backdrop of unjust oppression, and although the notion of unjust oppression no doubt assumes many guises, it is incomprehensible to me how we might understand it apart from the idea of the violation of basic moral rights.

What is true of human liberation is no less true of animal liberation. That the interests of nonhuman animals are not counted or, when they are, not counted equitably is a symptom, not the underlying cause, of their systematic exploitation. The fundamental wrong is the failure to respect their basic moral rights, including their rights to life, liberty, and bodily integrity. Moreover, as in the case of human slavery, so in the case of animal slavery: *the interests of those who profit from animal exploitation should play no role whatsoever in deciding whether to abolish the institution that furthers those interests.* It is only if or as humanity transforms itself and begins to respect the rights of other-than-human animals that anything like animal liberation can be achieved.

There is, then, I believe, a much better way to understand animal liberation than the one provided by an egalitarian interpretation of interests. It takes its cue from other kinds of liberation and rests the call for animal liberation on the recognition of the rights of nonhuman animals. When viewed in this light, animal liberation is the goal for which the philosophy of animal rights is the philosophy. The two—animal liberation and animal rights—go together like a hand in a vinyl glove.

Works Cited

Regan, Tom. 1983. *The Case for Animal Rights.* Berkeley: University of California Press.

Singer, Peter. 1975. *Animal Liberation.* New York: New York Review Books; dist. Random House.

3

THE CASE FOR ANIMAL RIGHTS:
A DECADE'S PASSING

During the academic year 1993–94 it was my honor to serve as president of the American Society for Value Inquiry (ASVI). The duties of this office are blessedly few; none is onerous, and all have the active support of the exceptional group of people who have made the society one of the jewels in philosophy's crown. I am very grateful to the members of ASVI not only for the professional honor they bestowed on me but also for motivating me to answer some of the more important objections raised against my book *The Case for Animal Rights*, first published in 1983.

The occasion to offer my answers was the society's annual Presidential Address, which I presented on December 29, 1993, in conjunction with the Eastern Division Meetings of the American Philosophical Association. Had it not been for the need to prepare something special for this event, I am not sure I would have taken up the issues I address in these pages. I certainly did not want to spend my life defending myself against the criticisms of others; like anyone with a glimmer of a creative spark, I wanted to explore new territory—new for me, in any event. I do not know whether I made a lasting contribution with the work I did during the decade after the publication of *The Case for Animal Rights*, much of it devoted to interpreting the moral philosophy of the early twentieth-century English philosopher G. E. Moore. What I do know, and what I knew at the time, is that I needed to step back from the animal rights debate for a good long while.

Along with several other contributing causes, the obligation to present the 1993 ASVI Presidential Address a decade after publication of *The Case for Animal Rights* proved to be incentive enough to revitalize my interest in that debate. As I note in my opening remarks, ten years has the feel of an anniversary. What better time, then, to undertake what I had been postponing? Although I could not reply to all my philosophical critics, I understood the obligation to reply to some. Indeed, without a willingness to respond to thoughtful critics, those who advocate a cause, whether animal rights or any other, risk sinking into unexamined zealotry, a charge often made against advocates of animal rights and one that I did not want to invite by remaining forever silent. For providing me with the occasion to offer my reply, and for much else besides, I wish to express my sincere gratitude to the officers, members, and traditions of the American Society for Value Inquiry.

"The Case for Animal Rights: A Decade's Passing" originally appeared in *A Quarter Century of Value Inquiry: Presidential Addresses of the American Society for Value Inquiry*, ed. Richard T. Hull, 439–59 (Amsterdam and Atlanta: Rodopi, 1994). Reprinted with the permission of the publisher.

❖

Ten years have now passed since the publication of *The Case for Animal Rights*. Sweet and bitter ink, generous and grim appraisals, and sympathetic and salacious sentiments have characterized the decade's responses. During this time I have read much, but not all, of what others have had to say, filing some of it away as worthy of reply and discarding the rest. Like any philosopher whose work is discussed and (even more) condemned, the temptation to respond has been both real and constant. With one notable exception (Regan 1991c), however, I have been able to resist, and—with what good results, others must decide—I have instead directed my attention elsewhere (Regan 1986a, 1986b, 1991b).

Anniversaries, however, even philosophical ones, should mean something, which is why I have decided to mark a decade's passing by using this unique occasion in my life as the time and place to answer some of my philosophical critics. I hope it is a proper choice. I especially hope it does not seem too self-indulgent. This is not my intention; rather, my intention is to help forward the general debate about the moral status of nonhuman animals— to help keep this debate alive and well. Before turning my attention to my critics, a few retrospective words about that one notable exception to which I have just alluded are in order.

"Animal rights" is more than a philosophical idea; it is also the name of a social-political movement: the animal rights movement. Ten million strong in the United States and among the fastest-growing progressive causes in America, this movement espouses uncompromisingly abolitionist goals; judged by contemporary standards, they may seem "radical" to most people, including most philosophers. The movement seeks, for example, to bring an end to the use of nonhuman animals in biomedical research rather than satisfy itself with increasing the size of laboratory cages. "Not larger cages," the movement declares, "empty cages." Understandably, those who speak for the world's powerful biomedical interests have challenged the idea of animal rights and the philosophy that informs it, just as, for reasons particular to their respective interests, representatives of the fur industry and the meat industry have publicly expressed their general disagreement with a philosophy that, were its goals to be achieved, would put them out of business.

All this is understandable—laudable, even. After all, truth should be decided on the basis of the fair, informed clash of ideas. If animal rightists bid the world listen to and act on the truth as they see it, it is only fitting and proper that the same opportunity should be made available to representatives of the Cattlemen's Association and the National Association for Biomedical Research. All of us who prize freedom of inquiry, and perhaps especially philosophers, should not only welcome critical public scrutiny of controversial ideas but insist on it.

In some hands, however, fairness is an ideal more honored in the breach than the observance. Throughout history, scurrilous attacks on the messenger have been a familiar way to attempt to discredit the message. So it is that, in lieu of competent criticism of my philosophical case for animal rights, some people in high places, both in and beyond academe, have slandered my character, for example, by accusing me of inciting others to riot during my campus lectures and by implicating me in the commission of a variety of violent crimes, including murder.

Now all this would be funny, in an Evelyn Waughish sort of way, if it were simply a case of a quixotic, graying moral philosopher tilting his blunt ideas against the resistant armor of powerful special interests. Given what I see as the real-life carnage at issue, however, it is not very funny at all. When one pauses to consider what, with the blessing of an indulgent culture, these special interests are in the business of doing—for example, there are more than ten thousand animals slaughtered for food every minute of every day just in the United States—the deliberate attempt to silence my voice by sullying my character is not a cause for laughter. Hence the need to respond to, rather than chuckle at, the ad hominem abuse that has been showered on me, a need I satisfied on the occasion to which I referred earlier. Happily, more recent work, by some members of the biomedical community in particular (Vance 1992), suggests that wiser, more temperate minds understand the need to confront the idea of animal rights on its merits rather than permit slander to substitute for rational argument. Whether an ethic more respectful of other animals will emerge as a result of this change in the respect accorded the idea of animal rights is unclear; what is clear is that such an ethic has little if any chance of emerging without such a change occurring, which is why, given my personal beliefs and aspirations, and notwithstanding the many obstacles still to be faced, I look on this change as a welcome development.

For their part, those philosophers who are to be counted among my critics have behaved beyond reproach. No name calling here. No threats or intimidation. No salacious rumors. No sullying of my reputation. Just good old-fashioned critical analysis. Wherever the truth lies, whether on my side of the debate or elsewhere, the principled manner in which both philosophical critics and philosophical defenders of animal rights have comported themselves, throughout the past ten years and more, gives philosophers reason to be proud of the high standards of our discipline and of the people who practice it.

As it happens, my philosophical critics are many; their specific objections, rich and diverse. At the most general level, however, they may be divided into two main groups. The first issues criticisms within a larger context of shared assumptions about the methods and objectives of moral philosophy. As is true in my own case, for example, these critics emphasize the role of reason in ethics as well as the legitimate roles played by moral principles— such principles as the categorical imperative or the principle of utility—that are at once abstract, universal, and impartial. The second group of critics goes further and challenges the very assumptions I share with the first group. The role of reason in ethics is challenged, for example, as is reliance on general moral principles. Those in the first group mount what we might term "intramoral" criticisms; those in the second, "intermoral." In what follows, after first giving a thumbnail sketch of my position, I consider representative examples of both. My objective throughout is not to consider all the criticisms that have been raised, or even to consider all the most important ones, since neither of these objectives could be realized on this occasion; my far more modest aim is to consider some of the most important criticisms of both types and to indicate how the challenges they pose might be addressed.

The Rights View

My position, roughly speaking, may be summarized as follows. Some nonhuman animals resemble normal humans in that, like us, they bring the mystery of a unified psychological presence to the world. Like us, they possess a variety of sensory, cognitive, conative, and volitional capacities. They see and hear, believe and desire, remember and anticipate, and plan and intend. Moreover, as is true in our case, what happens to them matters to them. Physical pleasure and pain—these they share with us. But they also share fear and contentment, anger and loneliness, frustration and satisfaction, and cunning and imprudence; these and a host of other psychological states and dispositions collectively help define the mental lives and relative well-being of those humans and animals who (in my terminology) are "subjects of a life."

In my view, subjects of a life have a basic moral right to respectful treatment. Of course, it is possible to advance moral positions that either dispense with rights altogether (Singer 1975) or, while affirming the rights of human beings, deny them in the case of nonhuman animals (Cohen 1986). But (or so I argue) any such theory will be deficient for one reason or another—for example, because it will be inconsistent or needlessly complicated, lack precision or adequate scope, or imply propositions that clash with a large body of our well-considered moral beliefs (our "intuitions"). When the competing ethical theories are thoroughly evaluated by reference to the appropriate standards, the rights view, as I call my position, emerges as the best theory.

The basic moral right to respectful treatment strictly limits how we may treat subject of a life. Individuals who possess this right are never to be treated as mere resources for others; in particular, harms intentionally done to any one subject cannot be justified by aggregating benefits derived by others. In this respect, my position is antiutilitarian, a theory in the Kantian, not the Millian, tradition. Nonetheless, my position parts company with Kant's when it comes to specifying *who* should be treated with respect. For Kant, only rational, autonomous persons are ends in themselves, a finding that excludes nonhuman animals (and, not unimportantly, many human beings as well), whereas on my position all subjects of a life, including all those nonhuman animals who qualify, have equal inherent value.

It is on this basis that I reach conclusions that, in Jan Narveson's cheerful words, qualify me as "a starry eyed radical" (Narveson 1987:38). In my view, since the utilization of nonhuman animals for purposes of, among other things, fashion, research, entertainment, or gustatory delight harms them and treats them as (our) resources, and since such treatment violates their right to be treated with respect, it follows that such utilization is morally wrong and ought to end. Merely to reform such institutional injustice (by resolving to eat only "happy" cows or to insist on larger cages, for example) is not enough. Morally considered, abolition is required.

That is roughly my position regarding the case for animal rights; I say something more about it later, as the occasion demands. Despite the many defects now evident to me in what I said and argued ten years ago, and notwithstanding the fact that, were I to write *The Case for Animal Rights* today, it would be a different book in certain respects, I continue to believe that the position presented and defended there is correct in its essential respects.

My critics are of a different mind; indeed, if they are right, I have secured for myself—by dint of my dogged persistence, so to speak—the unenviable distinction of being wrong about everything having the slightest presumption to philosophical importance. I am wrong about the minds of nonhuman animals, wrong about the way to evaluate moral theories, wrong about what rights are and who has them, wrong about what our moral duties are, and even wrong about what moral philosophy is and how to do it. With such a full plate of imputed failure, I must be selective in my responses. I begin with representative intramoral criticism.

Intramoral Critics

Among the objections raised by my intramoral critics, some concern my methodology, others concern elements in my theory of rights, and still others concern the theory's alleged implications. Jan Narveson (1987) objects to my methodology when he challenges my appeal to moral intuitions, R. G. Frey (1987) objects to elements in my theory when he criticizes my idea of inherent value, and Dale Jamieson (1990) objects to what he alleges are certain infelicitous implications of my theory. I will consider the objections in the order just given.

The Appeal to Intuition

How might we justify our acceptance of various moral principles, and how might we rationally choose among the conflicting moral theories of which these principles are a part? Anyone familiar with the history of moral philosophy knows how divisive and controversial these questions are. In *The Case for Animal Rights* I explain and attempt to defend a set of appropriate criteria for making such decisions. The criteria I deploy (Regan 1983b:131–47) are consistency, precision, scope, parsimony, and conformity with our intuitions. It is the last of these that has occasioned the most numerous critical responses, some of which, as I will illustrate shortly, are demonstrably ill focused.

Intuition is an ambiguous concept and a troublesome one no matter how it is understood. In *The Case*, after explaining several ways in which I do not understand it, I explain the sense of intuition I use as follows:

> The sense that is involved is what we shall term *the reflective sense*. In this sense, our intuitions are those moral beliefs we hold *after* we have made a conscientious effort . . . to think about our beliefs coolly, rationally, impartially, with conceptual clarity, and with as much relevant information as we can reasonably acquire. The judgments we make *after* we have made this effort are not our "gut responses," nor are they merely expressions of what we *happen* to believe; they are our *considered* beliefs. . . . To test alternative moral principles by how well they conform with our reflective intuitions is thus to test them against our considered beliefs, and, other things being equal between two competing moral principles (i.e., assuming that the two are equal in scope, precision, and consistency), the principle that matches our reflective intuitions best is rationally to be preferred. (Regan 1983b:134)

Having set forth how I understand the concept of intuition, I next go on to explain why some of our intuitions themselves might stand in need of revision or even abandonment if, as is possible, they conflict with principles that are otherwise validated. What we seek, in other words, is what Rawls (1971) refers to as "reflective equilibrium" between our intuitions, on the one hand, and our organizing general principles, on the other. Moreover—and here my theory becomes even more complicated than Rawls's and in some respects resembles ideal spectator views—I also explain why, given the ideal background conditions of arriving at our considered moral beliefs (impartiality, rationality, etc.), a proper humility should lead us to understand how elusive moral knowledge is. On my view, although we can be rationally *justified* in choosing one moral theory over others if we have done all that we can be reasonably expected to do by way of evaluating the competitors, it does not follow that we *know* the selected theory to be the only true one. What we can know, rather, is that we have done the best we are able to do in evaluating the theories fully and fairly with a view to deciding which one best satisfies the appropriate criteria, including the test of conforming with our moral intuitions. Given the previously mentioned background conditions, however, this last test represents an ideal that might never be realized despite our best efforts, so that we can never be justified in claiming to know that the favored theory is the only one that conforms with those considered beliefs we would have had we judged ideally.

Narveson is unhappy with my use of this methodology. Sometimes his consternation has my ideas as its object. More often than not, however, the objections he raises do not truly address my views, whether expressed or implied. For example, Narveson at one point makes light of my supposed belief that "the property" of inherent value is something I "intuit" (1987:38); at another place he takes exception to my supposed view that deciding who possesses inherent value is "a matter of moral perception" (39). Now, this may be an accurate way to characterize Moore's position regarding our acquaintance with the simple, unique, nonnatural property of intrinsic goodness his theory proposes, and it is true that I have written rather extensively about Moore's philosophy (Regan 1986a, 1986b, 1991b), but what Narveson says in the passages to which I have just alluded is manifestly an inaccurate way to characterize my own views. I have never claimed that "properties" (whatever they are) are "intuited" or that our intuitions are "a matter of moral perception" (whatever that is). To suppose otherwise is to do battle with someone other than the author of *The Case for Animal Rights.*

Narveson is not always this ill focused in his understanding of the way I understand moral intuitions. He writes correctly that when I appeal to intuitions, I am referring to "reflective intuitions, à la Sidgwick, Ross, and Rawls rather than sheer seat-of-the-pants pronouncements" (Narveson 1987:33). Even so, Narveson believes that when used as a basis for choosing between competing moral principles, the appeal to intuition "is theoretically bankrupt" (33) because "two mutually contradictory proposed moral principles could each pass it" (34). Thus, he asserts, passing this test "can't be sufficient" as a basis for justifying our acceptance of any one moral principle rather than another (34).

It should be plain, however, for reasons previously given, that I never assert or imply that conformity with our considered moral beliefs (our "moral intuitions") is a sufficient condition for choosing among moral principles or theories. The appeal to our intuitions is only one among a set of criteria of evaluation I deploy. If I thought passing the intuitive test to be sufficient, why would I bother to evaluate principles and theories against the demands of consistency, scope, precision, and simplicity? Clearly, my position entails that conformity with our intuitions constitutes only a *necessary* condition of adequacy, and it is no objection to this position to insist, as Narveson does, that passing this test cannot be sufficient. Moreover, although some of the theories I reject are criticized because they clash with a large body of moral intuitions, no theory is ever rejected on this ground alone; I always adduce some other reason logically distinct from appeals to intuitions (a lack of internal consistency is a recurring theme). In short, the appeal to moral intuitions does play a role in my evaluations of moral theories or principles, but only a limited one.

Still, it is appropriate to ask whether conformity with our moral intuitions should count as a necessary condition. Narveson arguably thinks not. Our intuitions, he seems to think, are just as likely as not to be expressions of our culturally biased times, places, and circumstances, which is why they should not be enlisted to do the rational and objective business of theory evaluation. I am not convinced that this is a mistake. Recall that, contrary to Narveson, the intuitions to which we are to appeal are not simply "hunch[es], or feeling[s], *that* a certain finding is the right one" (Narveson 1987:48). They are moral beliefs we form or retain after we have made a conscientious effort to think about them rationally, coolly, and impartially, assuming we understand the concepts involved and assuming we have secured as much relevant information as it is reasonable to demand. As I am at pains to explain, these conditions set forth an ideal that, imperfect creatures that we are, none of us may ever fully realize. Thus, as I noted earlier, although we can be rationally justified in accepting a given theory, it does not follow that we can therefore know that it is the only true one. Narveson might protest that he wants more; in particular, he might want to know which theory is "the true one." If the history of moral philosophy teaches us anything, however, it is that those who persist in searching for the one true theory are no more likely to meet with success than are those who, in the face of a record of unbroken failure, persist in hunting for the Snark—which, for the reasons already given, does not mean that we must view all moral theories as equally worthy of acceptance. Thus, although I am not so brazen as to suppose that my appeal to intuition is free of potentially serious difficulties, I do not believe Narveson, from whom I have learned much in other respects, whose work and wit I applaud, and whose friendship I value, has clearly identified what these might be.

The Idea of Inherent Value

Among my most persistent critics is R. G. Frey. In a series of articles and two books (Frey 1980, 1983), he argues against ascribing rights to nonhuman animals—and to humans. His is the stance of the unrepentant act utilitarian, an imperturbable partisan who, when confronted with the ghastly things his theory could permit, ranging from deceitful promises to the judicial execution of the innocent, tightens his grip on the theory rather than abandon it. Whereas the confidence of some philosophers might be shaken when it is pointed out that their favorite theory can have (literally) murderous consequences, Frey's commitment to utilitarianism does not waiver. Whatever else the shortcomings of his philosophy might be, Frey (a good friend of almost thirty years) is, if nothing else, consistent—in an Emersonian sense.

Frey does more than deny animals rights; he also denies them all but the faintest trace of mind. "Sensations," some pleasant, some painful, they can experience, but that is about it. They are barren of preferences, wants, and desires; they lack memory and expectation; and they are unable to reason, plan, or intend. Frey's conception of the mental life of nonhuman animals comes within a whisker, so to speak, of Descartes's. I have previously addressed this aspect of Frey's work and will not repeat my criticisms here (Regan 1983:38–53, 67–73). Instead I intend to consider his criticisms of an idea that is central to my theory of rights: inherent value.

To understand what this idea means and how it functions in my theory, inherent value needs to be seen in the larger context of all the sorts of values that play a role there. These values include (1) well-being (understood as quality of life, welfare, or happiness), (2) intrinsic values (including various mental states, such as pleasure and satisfaction), (3) utility (understood either as what is useful as a means, as what exists as a resource relative to someone's purposes or interests, as the aggregation of values such as welfare or pleasure), (4) merit or excellence, and (5) inherent value (understood as a kind of value possessed by certain individuals, after the fashion of Kant's idea of something's existing as an "end in itself").

Concerning inherent value, I argue four things. The first is that, although an ethical theory would be simpler if it could dispense with this kind of value, simplicity is not everything. To have the best theory, all things considered, we must postulate inherent value (here and throughout what follows, the Kantian echoes are evident to me now). Second, inherent value is logically distinct from, not reducible to, and not a function of the other kinds of values previously mentioned: a woman's moral status as an end in herself, as one who possesses inherent value, is logically independent of her happiness, talents, usefulness, and so on. Third, inherent value is a categorical concept, meaning that it does not come in degrees; an individual either has it or not, and all those who have inherent value have it equally. (To express these points in Kantian terms, one would say that a given man either exists as an end in himself or does not, and all those who exist as ends in themselves have this status equally). Fourth, all those individuals who are subjects of a life have inherent value and thus enjoy an equal moral status, the

subject-of-a-life criterion constituting a sufficient condition for the possession of inherent value.

Many critics have taken exception to the idea of inherent value, Frey
among them. He disputes both the idea itself and its alleged equality. Concerning the former, Frey informs his readers:

> I do not regard all human life as of equal value; I do not accept that a
> very severely mentally-enfeebled human or an elderly human fully in the
> grip of senile dementia or an infant born with only half a brain has a life
> whose value is equal to that of normal, adult humans. The quality of
> human life can plummet, to a point where we would not wish *that* life
> on even our worst enemies; and I see no reason to pretend that a life I
> would not wish upon even my worst enemies is nevertheless as valuable
> as the life of any normal, adult human. (Frey 1987:58)

Notice that in the passage just quoted, Frey refers to the *quality* of human life and to the fact that it can vary from individual to individual, sometimes plummeting to an unquestionably undesirable level. It should be clear,
however, that in challenging my position in the way he does, Frey has confused the idea of inherent value with the very different idea of individual
welfare. To speak of quality of life is to refer to how well an individual's life
is faring, while to speak of the inherent value of an individual is to refer to
the value (the moral status) of the individual whose life it is. Individuals who
are confused, enfeebled, or otherwise disadvantaged, let us agree, have lives
that are of a lesser quality than the life of someone who realizes the highest
level on Maslow's scale of self-actualization. But this does not entail that
those with a lesser quality of life lack inherent value or that they may with
moral justification be treated as mere resources by those who have a better
quality of life. Not for a moment do I deny that the experiential welfare of
different individuals can vary greatly. But as I have never said or implied that
it is everywhere the same, Frey's insistence that it can vary fails to mount a
criticism against my position.

The same is true of Frey's comments about my views regarding the equality of inherent value. After first (falsely) attributing to me the position that
"all human life, however deficient, has the same value," he continues: "I do
not agree. For me, the value of life is a function of its quality, its quality a
function of its richness, and its richness a function of its scope or potential-
ity for enrichment; and the fact is that many humans lead lives of a very much
lower quality than ordinary human lives, lives which lack enrichment and
where the potentialities for enrichment are severely truncated or absent"

(1987:57). Once again, however, Frey does not so much challenge my views as miss what they are. First, I do not state or imply that "all human life . . . has the same value," including the same inherent value (because not all human beings satisfy the subject-of-a-life criterion); second, although all humans who satisfy this criterion in my view have inherent value and have it equally, it does not follow that the quality of their lives is equal. In short, given my theory of value, the quality of an individual's life is one thing; the value of the one living that life is another. Since Frey treats the two ideas as if they were the same, his protestations misfire.

Duties of Assistance

Any theory of rights is obliged to consider what we owe by way of assistance. The position I offer in *The Case for Animal Rights* is that we do not exhaust our duties of justice simply by seeing to it that we personally have not violated the rights of others; we also have a prima facie duty to assist those individuals who are victims of injustice—in other words, individuals who have had their rights violated.

Dale Jamieson (1990) challenges what he takes to be some of the implications of this part of my theory. Noting that, in my view, only moral agents can violate another's rights, he argues that "although [according to Regan] we are required to assist those who are victims of injustice, we are not required to help those in need who are not victims of injustice" (351). He refers to my discussion of various wildlife issues and quotes the following passage from *The Case for Animal Rights:* "In claiming that we have a prima facie duty to assist those animals *whose rights have been violated* . . . , we are not claiming that we have a duty to assist the sheep against the attack of the wolf, since the wolf neither can nor does violate anyone's rights" (Regan 1983b:285). He then argues that my position regarding duties of assistance has counterintuitive consequences. For example, it seems to imply that we have no duty to warn a fellow hiker that a boulder is heading his way if the danger does not result from human wrongdoing. After all, according to Jamieson, my position holds that "we are not required to help those in need who are not victims of injustice." And free-falling boulders, whatever else might be said of them, are not agents of injustice.

Despite its initial appearance as a potentially serious objection, I do not think Jamieson's criticism stands up. A careful reading of the relevant passages shows that I do not maintain what Jamieson imagines that I do; in particular, I do not maintain that we owe nothing to those in need who are not victims of injustice. What I do maintain is that we do not owe anything to such individuals *on the grounds of justice*. Thus, there is nothing in my theory that would preclude recognizing a duty to warn the hiker about the free-falling boulder; the point is only that we owe the warning for reasons other than the demands of justice, for free-falling boulders violate no one's rights.

Jamieson anticipates that I might respond in this way and explains why he thinks I cannot. He writes that my theory "does not recognize nondiscretionary duties of assistance that are not duties of justice" (1990:354). Now I am not sure I understand what Jamieson means by "nondiscretionary duty"; this is not a concept I use, and it is not one that he explains. If he means that it is not up to individuals to decide whether they have duties of assistance to the victims of injustice, then what he says is true of my position, but if he means that it is not up to individuals to decide how and when and to what extent to try to discharge such duties, then what he says is not true of my position. My position, in other words, is that we are not at liberty to decide whether we have such duties, but we are at liberty to decide how to discharge them. I will assume that this is how Jamieson understands the matter. Moreover, I will be the first to concede that, among the nondiscretionary duties of assistance mentioned in *The Case for Animal Rights*, only duties based on respect for justice are mentioned explicitly.

As Jamieson should well know, however, I take pains to emphasize that "the rights view is not a complete theory in its present form" (Regan 1983b:xiv). Unless there is some principled reason for blocking my possible recognition of duties of assistance in addition to those based on duties of justice, Jamieson's objection will fail to carry the day.

Jamieson evidently thinks he has such a reason when he suggests that any response I might give cannot merely be "ad hoc," a response intended "to postulate . . . a class of duties simply to circumvent problems posed by the boulder cases" (1990:354). Whatever the basis for such duties might be, Jamieson believes that "it must mark some important difference between duties of justice and other nondiscretionary duties" (ibid.).

I am not sure I understand the dilemma Jamieson imagines I must face. If I were to say that duties of assistance depend on duties of justice except when God commands otherwise, in which case one should help anyhow, then I can easily imagine how someone might dismiss my defense as ad hoc. Other possible responses, however, without being ad hoc, seem to be perfectly consistent with the general theory of respect for the individual I promulgate. Specifically, I might reply that we have a prima facie duty of beneficence, a duty that includes lending meaningful assistance to those who need it through no fault of their own and that obligates us independently of any question of their rights being violated. I do not see why or how this constitutes an "ad hoc" reply or why, in the particular case of the falling boulder, my position prevents me from saying that we ought to discharge this duty by warning the hiker.

Jamieson seems to imagine that such a response would merely thicken the plot, not resolve it, for he seems to think that the issue would then become the stringency of the duty to assist those in need who are not victims of injustice. But this is to strain at gnats. I am not aware of any plausible moral theory that is able to specify, in advance, *exactly when, where, and how* everyone is supposed to discharge the duties of assistance we owe to one another. Indeed, as noted earlier, although individuals are not free to decide whether they have such duties, they are free to decide when, where, and how to discharge them. To expect more from a moral theory than this—to expect it to specify, in advance of real-life circumstances, and for all people at all times and in all places—when, where, and how they are to assist others is ludicrous on its face. The crucial point (and the final one I will make as I conclude my discussion of Jamieson's objections) is that duties of assistance must conform to the demands of the fundamental principles of justice that define my theory. In other words, we can never have a duty to assist someone in ways that involve treating others with a lack of respect. In this regard, there is a moral limit to how much discretion we have in deciding whom we should help and how we can help them.

Intermoral Critics

Theories of individual moral rights, even when their scope is limited to rational, autonomous persons, are fraught with deep, abiding difficulties. The challenge to such theories raised by some utilitarians (Hare 1978) is a familiar one. As for animal rights theory, the critics include such widely divergent voices as those of Kantians, contractarians, and libertarians. As noted earlier, however, despite their substantive differences, these approaches to moral philosophy have important similarities. At the level of theory, the object of moral philosophy is essentially the same: to explain and defend the fundamental principle or principles of morality, principles that will be general, abstract, and impartial. At the level of practice, moreover, these theorists share a common vision: the right thing to do, they all seem to imply, in most if not all cases, is to be determined by assessing what an informed application of the favored principle(s) would have us do given the details of the situation. Philosophers who share these theoretical and practical outlooks obviously can and frequently do differ with one another over what the fundamental principles of morality are and what we should do in particular cases. In fact, the previously considered criticisms of my views illustrate this point. Narveson, Frey, Jamieson, and I disagree about a great many things, both at the level of theory and at the level of practice, but we do not disagree about what we as moral theorists are trying to do or the way we think people should try to determine what ought to be done.

Such are the resources of moral philosophy, however, that new channels of thought are constantly being opened and explored. It should hardly be surprising, therefore, that in addition to such intramoral criticisms of animal rights as those I have considered, new and significantly different criticisms directed at the very assumptions evident both in my own work and in the work of my intramoral challengers need to be considered. It is to a consideration of one such line of criticism that I now turn.

According to the criticism I have in mind, Narveson, Frey, and Jamieson are correct insofar as they hold that there is something seriously mistaken in the view that nonhuman animals have rights. But they are mistaken when it comes to explaining why the idea is ill grounded. The fault lies in the very idea of the rights of the individual. This idea, these critics allege, is symptomatic of a deep, systematic prejudice that has distorted Western moral and political thought down through the ages. That prejudice is patriarchy, understood as what is expressive of male bias. Paradoxical though it may seem, they claim that what is fundamentally wrong with the idea of animal rights is that it encapsulates male bias. Before moving on to explore this criticism (which for brevity's sake I term "the feminist indictment"), three preliminary points merit mention.

First, not all those philosophers who consider themselves feminists accept the view that the idea of individual rights bespeaks patriarchal bias; indeed, some feminists (so-called liberal feminists) strenuously deny it (Regan 1991a). Second, whether accepted or rejected, the indictment, as I have tried to indicate, is perfectly general in scope. It does not allege merely that *some* views about individual rights are patriarchal; *all* views about the rights of the individual, whether or not the individual is a human being, are allegedly tainted by male bias. Third, the feminist indictment regarding individual rights can be seen as part of a larger critique of the way both my intramoral critics and I understand moral philosophy. As I will explain later, at its deepest level the feminist indictment attacks this way of doing moral philosophy as itself being patriarchal.

How might one attempt to defend the view that the idea of individual rights is patriarchal? My examination of answers to this question lays no claim to completeness. I am able to consider only three possible responses. To the best of my knowledge, the first two, while common enough, have not surfaced in the philosophical literature (they are more in the nature of popular argument); the third surfaces frequently, however, and is by far the most important of the three responses to be considered.

The Genealogy Defense

One possible defense of the feminist indictment appeals to the genealogy of the idea of individual rights. After all, it was men who first formulated this idea—the Lockes and Rousseaus of the world, not the Xanthippes and Hildegards. The genealogy defense (to give this line of reasoning a name) would have us infer that an idea is patriarchal if it was originated by men.

This is an implausible defense. If we were to accept it, we would be obliged to say that our current understanding of the circulation of blood is patriarchal because it was Harvey and his male contemporaries who were the first to discover how blood circulates. No less absurd consequences would follow in every other similar context (for example, Euclidean geometry must be patriarchal because Euclid was a man). Surely it is absurd to imagine that Euclid's definition of a right triangle is a symptom of male domination or that it arbitrarily favors, or favors in any way whatsoever, the interests of men over those of women. Logically, the fact that a man discovers, creates, or simply says something does not entail that what is discovered, created, or said is tainted by male prejudice.

The Implementation Defense

A second possible defense of the feminist indictment, the implementation defense, takes a different route. Even a cursory view of social history, from classical Greek civilization up to the present, confirms that by claiming rights for themselves, men have routinely received advantages that have been routinely and systematically denied to women (Regan 2000). No less clearly, men have overwhelmingly been the ones to decide who is to be the beneficiary of these advantages. Thus, because reliance on the idea of individual rights can be shown to have these patriarchal results, should we not conclude that the very idea of individual rights itself is patriarchal?

It seems not. Ideas are not shown to be patriarchal simply because they have been used in a patriarchal fashion; if anything, the patriarchal use of ideas shows that those who use them are patriarchal, not that the ideas them-selves are. To make this point clearer, consider an example from another quarter. Various people over time have used the idea of genetic inheritance as a basis for classifying the members of some race "superior" and others "inferior." Does this show that the idea of genetic inheritance is a racist idea? Clearly not. What it shows is something very different—namely, that some people have used the idea of genetic inheritance in a racist fashion.

The same is true of individual rights. One cannot logically infer that the idea of the rights of the individual is tainted with male bias because biased men have used it to forward their interests at the expense of women's.

The Male Mind Defense

A third, more subtle defense of the feminist indictment (the last I will con-sider) takes the following form (Regan 1991a). Owing to a variety of cultur-al forces, it is alleged, men in general tend to think in certain ways; women, in others. This defense avers that men tend to think in dualistic, hierarchi-cal terms. For example, they tend to view reason as standing against emo-tion (a dualism) and to think that reason is the superior of the two (a hierar-chy). This same pattern emerges in the cases of objectivity and subjectivity, impartiality and partiality, justice and care, culture and nature, and individ-ualism and communitarianism; in each of these and other cases, men tend to carve up the world in dualistic terms, and in each such case, one of the two terms is ranked higher, as being of greater importance or value, than its complement.

What we might term "male mind," then, is characterized by the dualis-tic, hierarchical rankings men tend to make—or so it is alleged—a summary of which would read as follows. Men tend to believe that reason, objectivity, impartiality, justice, culture, and individualism are of greater importance or value than emotion, subjectivity, partiality, care, nature, and community. Moreover, men also tend to think that men are characterized by the higher-ranked item in each of the dualisms, and women by the lower. Thus women are supposed (by men) to be less rational and more emotional, less objective and more subjective, and so on.

With the preceding sketch serving as logical backdrop, the male mind defense of the feminist indictment comes to this: the idea of the rights of the individual is a product of male mind and thus of male bias. It is a prod-uct of male mind because, for example, it grows out of a conception of the world that places greater value on the separateness of the individual (the rights, after all, are the rights of the *individual*) than on familial and communitarian relationships, and it places greater importance on evaluating moral choices in terms of impartial considerations, such as justice, than on evaluating them in terms of our responsibility to care for (to nurture and sustain) close interpersonal relationships, such as the relationships that obtain between parents and their children. The moral significance of these latter relationships is denigrated by male mind; they are, as it were, "women's work" and thus of less importance than the acts or policies that honor the universal, equal, inalienable rights of the individual. Against this judgment, partisans of the male mind defense celebrate the qualities (for example, emotion, subjectivity, and an ethic of care) traditionally associated with the feminine.

But the scope of the male mind defense extends beyond the particular idea of "the rights of the individual." This defense bears the seeds of a more general indictment of the way moral philosophy has been and continues to be done by many theorists. To persist in searching for moral principles that are at once universal, abstract, and impartial, as my intramoral critics and I persist in doing, is implicitly to bespeak the patriarchal prejudices definitive of male mind.

Now there is, I think, much that is unclear in the preceding account. The concepts used to describe male mind are so general and vague that it seems the better part of wisdom to withhold judgment of the idea's validity until a much fuller, more precise story has been told. I will have more (but not enough) to say on this topic later. These matters to one side, what may be said for and against the male mind defense? I will consider five areas of controversy. The first is empirical and concerns disputes about the evidence for the portrait of patriarchy sketched previously; the second concerns the paradoxical presuppositions of the male mind defense; the third and fourth challenge the alleged shortcomings of "hierarchical" thinking; and the fifth explores, albeit incompletely, the way some feminist theorists have used elements of the male mind defense to criticize my position regarding animal rights.

The Empirical Debate The pioneering work of developmental psychologist Carol Gilligan (1982, 1987) is central to the male mind defense. Initially a research associate of Lawrence Kohlberg, Gilligan in time came to wonder why females tended to score lower on Kohlberg's scale for measuring moral development, a scale that awarded a higher ranking to those who relied on abstract, universal, and impartial moral principles (Kohlberg 1984). Rather than view Kohlberg's various stages as constituting an objective, non-question-begging map of moral development, Gilligan became convinced that the philosophy underlying Kohlberg's various stages masks a variety of male biases. In her earlier work she suggests that both the "justice" and "care" orientations are needed and that both play a role in the morally mature person; more recently she has suggested that most women approach moral choice from the care perspective, while most men go about the business of making moral decisions from the justice perspective. Even so, Gilligan herself does not claim that care is better than justice, except insofar as she believes that the justice perspective is more apt to engender violence, including nuclear war; in this respect she implies that an ethic of care is superior to an ethic of justice.

Not all Gilligan's readers have been as willing to accept her findings as have proponents of the male mind defense. In particular, some critics have questioned Gilligan's methodology (Larrabee 1993) and the prima facie unrepresentative character of her research subjects, many being the well-educated children of wealthy white parents. A more provocative challenge, one having its origins in the emerging work of Africanists such as economist Vern Dixon (1976), questions the genderization of the care/justice debate. Dixon and others argue that the ethical orientation of African men is strikingly similar to that of Euro-American women; the former, like the latter, are more concerned with sustaining intimate personal relationships and less interested in asserting individual autonomy. One could argue, of course, that both African men and Euro-American women have forged this ethical orientation in response to their domination by white men of European ancestry, but to push this line of reasoning is tantamount to abandoning the male mind defense of the feminist indictment. That the care perspective is widely shared among African men seems to suggest that *there is nothing distinctively female in that perspective*, any more than there is anything distinctively male in the justice perspective. At the very least, we would all do well to question the empirical basis for the contrary judgments.

The Paradox In addition to facing legitimate concerns about its empirical underpinnings, the male mind defense also seems to confront a damaging paradox of its own making. Notwithstanding its purported attack on patriarchy, the male mind defense arguably bears symptoms of the very prejudice it seeks first to expose and then to supplant. Partisans of this defense not only denounce the valorization of those qualities that they claim have been traditionally associated with the masculine; they also celebrate those qualities (emotion, subjectivity, an ethic of care) traditionally associated with the feminine. Yet the implied claim to superiority on behalf of these feminine qualities appears highly paradoxical, first, because celebrating the "feminine" set of qualities over the masculine is to engage in the very sort of dualistic, hierarchical thinking alleged to be characteristic of male mind, and second, because the collective portrait of those qualities that are definitive of the female, like every other portrait in the patriarchy, will have been drawn not by women but by men. How paradoxical, then, that pursuant to their liberation from the crippling vestiges of patriarchy, some women should choose to define themselves in the very terms in which they have been defined by the patriarchal traditions they seek to overthrow.

Reason and Emotion A third issue meriting attention concerns the alleged dualism and hierarchy of reason and emotion. It is unquestionably true, I think, that most male philosophers have ranked the capacity to reason in some sense above the capacity to feel emotions. In this respect, Locke is the rule, not the exception. Recall how, on his view, we humans have the natural rights we do because we are rational and autonomous, not because we can feel pity or sorrow. It is also true that in the broad sweep of Western customs and attitudes, women in general have been viewed as being less rational and more emotional than men (Regan 1999).

Nevertheless, these facts, assuming them to be so, do not establish that patriarchal prejudice is implicit when reason is placed above emotion. For rationality *just might be* a more important feature of being human than are the capacities to feel sorrow or anger. That question remains open. To suppose that it is closed because men have tended to rank reason above emotion is again mistakenly to infer something about the content of an idea from facts about its genealogy (like inferring that the concept of a right triangle is patriarchal because men were the first to define it). Notice, too, that it would also be a mistake to infer that the traditional ranking of reason over emotion must be patriarchal because men, in claiming greater rational capacity for themselves, have claimed rights on their behalf that have been denied to women. This latter fact does not support the view that it is patriarchal to base the possession of rights on the capacity to reason; at most it supports the very different view that men have acted in patriarchal ways in implementing respect for women's' rights because of their (men's) mistaken beliefs about the lack of reason in women—a truly lamentable legacy, let it be granted, but one that does not offer evidence of patriarchal bias in the very idea of the rights of the individual.

But it may be asked, why suppose that the capacity to reason should be ranked "higher" than the capacity to feel emotions? A thorough discussion of this question would be obliged carefully to explain and assess the assumption that the two capacities really are as distinct as the question assumes. Possibly they are; possibly they are not. On this occasion I can offer only some tentative, impressionistic reasons for thinking that they are distinct. Similarly, my discussion of why and in what sense the capacity to reason might be ranked above the capacity to feel emotions is quite limited, consisting only of the following observations concerning the role reason, broadly construed, often plays in assessing the appropriateness of our emotions.

Experience teaches that our feelings sometimes are inappropriate because they are based on mistaken beliefs. I well remember, for example, hearing a young man sing the *Star-Spangled Banner* on the radio at the start of a Durham Bulls baseball game. Musically it was a disaster. By contrast, Roseanne Barr's fabled rendition of this song was the equal of a Beverley Sills's aria. It was so bad that I laughed out loud. After the song ended, however, and the announcer explained that the young singer suffered from serious physical and mental disabilities, what I initially found funny turned serious. An aura of courage now surrounded the performance. My feelings changed because my beliefs changed. What I had felt emerged as inappropriate to what had taken place, something I came to understand not by feeling my way through the world, as it were, but by using ordinary ways of knowing—ways that involve the elementary application of reason.

We have all had similar experiences, and most of us have had them not rarely but fairly often. Moreover, most of us are familiar with the process by which we come to recognize that our feelings (for example, about members of religions or races other than our own) are grounded in beliefs that we have accepted uncritically (for example, the belief that Native Americans are lazy and shiftless). Once we see through the prejudicial character of such beliefs, the feelings we have toward others (for example, Gentiles' feelings about Jews, or Caucasians' feelings about African Americans) can and often do change. Throughout this process our capacity to reason is called on to play a role that our capacity to feel cannot perform.

More generally, emotions without reason can be blind. The task of checking the factual and inferential basis of the emotions we feel exceeds both the reach and the grasp of our power to feel them. In a very real sense, this is part of the human condition. How, then, can it plausibly be judged to be patriarchal to recognize the limits of emotion or the role of reason in this regard? We do not denigrate the importance of emotions in human life if we rank reason "above" emotion. For my part, then, I am not convinced that recognizing a dualism or hierarchy between reason and emotion is a bad thing in general or a symptom of male domination in particular.

Justice and Care As I have mentioned, another dualistic hierarchy cited in the male mind defense concerns the distinction between justice and care. We understand justice as giving everyone her or his due—or alternatively, as treating others as they deserve to be treated. Understood in this sense, justice and individual rights are companion concepts: if people have a right to be treated in certain ways, they deserve to be treated in those ways; such treatment is something to which they are entitled, something they can claim as their due, *as a matter of justice*. The concept of care differs from this. Care is something that is freely given—for example, as an expression of love, friendship, or compassion—not extracted from another as something that is due, after the fashion of a debt owed. To care for others is to be disposed to act to forward their interests whether or not they deserve such concern. The most important and intimate of human relations—for example, those between parents and their children, between friends, or between lovers— are expressions of the human capacity to care, not responses to the impersonal demands of abstract justice.

The male mind defense posits that men in general are inclined to understand morality in terms of justice; women, in terms of care. Thus it is claimed that because the ethic of justice is inextricably connected with the idea of the rights of the individual, that idea bears the imprint of male mind and thus of patriarchy. How strong is this defense of the feminist indictment?

To begin with, it is difficult to understand how anyone can doubt that there is a real difference between the concepts of justice and care. Justice is something we can demand as our right; care is not. Indeed, if things were otherwise—if care were something we could demand as an individual right— then, contrary to the male mind defense, the ethic of care would also be patriarchal, since it, too, would be built on and incorporate the idea of the rights of the individual. Both partisans and critics of the male mind defense, then, should agree that justice and care, and their respective moral directives, differ in the crucial respects I have noted.

Empirically considered, the situation is far less clear. Certainly it is possible that men are inclined to think about moral responsibility in terms of justice and individual rights, and that women are inclined to do so in terms of care. Some psychological studies seem to support this finding. The number of relevant studies conducted to date is small, however, and those that have been done are less than conclusive. To the extent that the male mind defense stands or falls on the relevant empirical data at hand, those who are not already committed to the feminist indictment are well advised to withhold their informed assent.

There is an alternative way to regard the apparent conflict between interpreting moral responsibility in ways that emphasize justice and doing so in ways that emphasize care. This is to view the apparent conflict as normative in character rather than empirical—that is, as a conflict not between how men and women *as a matter of fact* tend to understand moral responsibility but between two conflicting interpretations of how all of us, men and women alike, *ought* to understand it. When viewed in this way, the relative scarcity of empirical data concerning typical male and typical female moral development becomes moot. The issue now concerns which type of ethic is superior as an ethic, whatever may be psychologically true of current patterns of male and female moral thinking.

Now, it seems to me that any fully credible ethic will have to find a place for both justice and care. Consider care first. While it is doubtless true that parents have duties to their children, and that many fail miserably in discharging them, it is no less true that parental character is improved to the extent that parents are motivated by their care for their children, rather than by their choice to conform their wills to abstract principles of justice. Kant, it is true, teaches that one's moral worth is contingent on one's capacity to do one's duty for duty's sake, especially when tempted to act otherwise. On this matter, however, Aristotle seems closer to the truth: the best parent is one who does good by her or his child out of love and concern for the child and in the absence of any desire to do less. In this respect, as well as in others, the importance, indeed the centrality, of care in a fully developed moral life seems too obvious to require further support.

The same is no less true of the role of justice. Morally speaking, care is not enough. And it is not enough because it is too limited. The plain fact is that most people care too little about too few people. The circle of care may include some family members, friends, a few neighbors, and maybe some business associates. The list is not long by any means. If the boundaries of moral responsibility are fixed by those relationships of care that people actually have, then people will be free to deny any sense of responsibility to those who stand outside the circle of their caring relationships (i.e., the overwhelmingly greater part of humanity). Do white racists have any moral responsibilities to Asians and Chicanos? Given the present interpretation of the ethic of care, it seems not; after all, they fail to care for them. The absence of care, it seems, means the absence of responsibility. This does not bode well for an ethic of care as here interpreted.

A possible response is that people *should* care for others—indeed, that we should care for *everyone*—even if we happen not to do so. In particular, we should care for all those who are the victims of oppression: children, members of racial minorities, homosexuals, the poor, women, possibly even nonhuman animals. Understood in this way, the ethic of care can hardly be faulted for being morally conservative; only now serious questions arise about its internal consistency. If the ethic bids us to act in caring ways toward everyone, not just family members and friends, then this ethic's guiding principle ("Act caringly toward everyone") looks very much like the sort of patriarchal ethic allegedly associated with male mind—a principle that is at once abstract, universal, objective, and impartial.

Thus it is that proponents of an ethic of care face what is to my mind an insuperable dilemma: either the ethic is grounded in the limited, partial care that people do have for others, in which case its implications are friendly to the worst forms of moral prejudices (including prejudices against women), or the ethic is grounded in an unlimited, impartial care for everyone, in which case it takes its place alongside other ethics that advocate universal, abstract principles (and by implication embodies some of the very attributes of patriarchal ethics it seeks to expose and overcome). The choice, that is, is between a morally inadequate ethic or a logically inconsistent one.

Patriarchy and Animal Rights Much of the feminist criticism of my position takes a predictable form. Patriarchal modes of thought are first characterized in terms of certain traits (a, b, and c); my position is said to have traits a, b, and c; therefore, my position is denounced as patriarchal. Thus, Deborah Slicer (1991) writes that my ethical theory is typical of "the justice tradition" (110), that it "perpetuates . . . our culture's objectionable use of dualistic hierarchies" (112), that it embodies "a masculine sense of the self" (for example, insofar as it incorporates a "masculinist contempt for our emotions" [115]), and that it would have us "worship principles while neglecting such things as virtues and the affections" (113). My views are said to "grossly oversimplify" (114) the moral issues they aspire to address; in some cases these views are said to be "dangerously misleading" (109).

In much the same mode Josephine Donovon (1993) writes disparagingly of my "determined exclusion of sentiment from 'serious' intellectual inquiry" (170) and of the way my position "privileges rationalism and individualism" (ibid.), noting the need for "a critique of the atomistic individualism and rationalism of the liberal tradition . . . , a vision that emphasize[s] collectivity, emotional bonding, and an organic (or holistic) concept of life" (173). When all the dust settles, the philosophy one gets in *The Case for Animal Rights* is, in Donovon's word, "biased" (168).

In view of my previous comments on the debate surrounding the empirical basis of the male mind defense and the self-inflicted paradox to which this defense is heir, I hope it is clear that Slicer's and Donovon's dismissive characterizations of my views assume the greater part of what needs to be established. For example, if there is nothing essentially "masculinist" about an ethic in "the justice tradition," then while it may be ideologically correct to chastise my views as "masculinist," the question of the nonideological accuracy of such descriptions remains open. Moreover, it is relevant to ask how fair these critics are in their efforts to understand and characterize the views they attribute to me. A few examples will show that fairness sometimes is a scarce commodity.

—My views are said to display "the masculinist contempt for emotion." The sole evidence given for this judgment is my insistence that the case for animal rights I present relies on reason, not emotion. How could it be otherwise? How, that is, could one conceivably offer a theory of animal rights based on appeals to emotion? What could such a theory possibly maintain? The claim that emotion has its limits hardly expresses contempt for emotion, and it is the thesis that emotion has its limits, not contempt for emotion, that one finds in my work.

—Consider, further, the following passage from an essay of mine that has been readily accessible for the better part of ten years: "There are times, and these not infrequent, when tears come to my eyes when I see, or read, or hear of the wretched plight of animals in the hands of humans. Their pain, their suffering, their loneliness, their innocence, their death. Anger. Rage. Pity. Sorrow. Disgust. . . . It *is* our hearts, not just our heads, that call for an end to it all" (Regan 1985:25). How, I wonder, can one read a passage like this one and criticize me for harboring a masculinist contempt for emotion?

—I am said to offer an approach to ethics that "worships principles while neglecting such things as virtue or the affections," despite the fact that I have published a lengthy refutation of utilitarianism (Regan 1983a) based on this theory's inability to account for the great value friendship has in human life.

And so it goes. I do not claim that Slicer, Donovon, and other feminist critics of my position willfully or maliciously misrepresent my ideas. I claim only that they do misrepresent them, not rarely, but often. By itself, of course, this does not make my ideas any more credible than they otherwise might be. Nonetheless, when added to the reasons I have presented on previous occasions (Regan 1991a), it does go some way toward explaining why I do not believe the feminist critique of the philosophy of animal rights, as reviewed on this occasion, is compelling enough to require modifying or rejecting my position.

Conclusion

It has not been my intention to reargue the full case for animal rights or even to respond to all the most important criticisms that have been raised against the case as originally presented some ten years ago. I have been obliged to be selective in choosing what to consider. However, I have made my selections with a view to highlighting, in the most general way, the sorts of objections a more complete response would need to consider. Some of these objections are intramoral; others, intermoral. The former raise various objections within the larger context of shared assumptions about the nature and purpose of ethical theory; the latter challenge these very assumptions. Among the former, some challenge the methodology used in developing my theory of rights; some, the terms of the theory itself; and some, the alleged implications of the theory. Representative of the latter is the challenge embodied in the feminist indictment. I am not certain whether I have responded fairly and well to the specific criticisms I have discussed; I know I have not responded fully. Perhaps the future will permit the opportunity for a more leisurely exploration. The one thing that is clear, is the heavy debt I owe to all those who have taken the time to read my work and to challenge me to do better. To all these, my informed, fair critics, both those whom I have been able to consider on this occasion and those whose objections await some possible future airing, I conclude by saying, "Thank you."

Works Cited

Cohen, Carl. 1986. "The Case for the Use of Animals in Biomedical Research." *New England Journal of Medicine* 315, no. 14 (Oct. 2): 865–70.

Dixon, Vern. 1976. "World Views and Research Methodology." In *African Philosophy: Assumptions and Paradigms for Research on Black Persons*, ed. L. M. King, V. Dixon, and W. W. Nobles. Los Angeles: Charles R. Drew Postgraduate Medical School, Fanon Center.

Donovon, Josephine. 1993. "Animal Rights and Feminist Theory." In *Ecofeminism:*

Women, Animals, Nature, ed. Greta Gaard, 167–94. Philadelphia: Temple University Press.

Frey, R. G. 1980. *Interests and Rights: The Case against Animals*. Oxford: Oxford University Press.

———. 1983. *Rights, Killing, and Suffering*. Oxford: Blackwell.

———. 1987. "Autonomy and the Value of Animal Life." *Monist* 70, no. 1:50–63.

Gilligan, Carol. 1982. *In a Different Voice: Psychological Theory and Women's Development*. Cambridge, Mass.: Harvard University Press.

———. 1987. "Moral Orientation and Moral Development." In *Women and Moral Theory*, ed. Eva Feder Kitay and Diana T. Meyers, 19–36. Totowa, N.J.: Rowman and Littlefield.

Hare, R. M. 1978. "Justice and Equality." In *Justice and Economic Distribution*, ed. John Arthur and William H. Shaw, 16–31. Englewood Cliffs, N.J.: Prentice-Hall.

Jamieson, Dale. 1990. "Rights, Justice, and Duties to Provide Assistance: A Critique of Regan's Theory of Rights." *Ethics* 100, no. 1:349–62.

Kohlberg, Lawrence. 1984. *The Psychology of Moral Development*. San Francisco: Harper and Row.

Larrabee, Mary Jeanne, ed. 1993. *An Ethic of Care: Feminist and Interdisciplinary Perspectives*. New York: Routledge, Chapman and Hall.

Narveson, Jan. 1987. "On a Case for Animal Rights." *Monist* 70, no. 1:31–49.

Rawls, John. 1971. *A Theory of Justice*. Cambridge, Mass.: Harvard University Press.

Regan, Tom. 1983a. "A Refutation of Utilitarianism." *Canadian Journal of Philosophy* 13, no. 2:141–59.

———. 1983b. *The Case for Animal Rights*. Berkeley: University of California Press.

———. 1985. "The Case for Animal Rights." In *In Defense of Animals*, ed. Peter Singer, 13–26. Oxford: Blackwell.

———. 1986a. *Bloomsbury's Prophet: G. E. Moore and the Development of His Moral Philosophy*. Philadelphia: Temple University Press.

———, ed. 1986b. *Moore: The Early Essays*. Philadelphia: Temple University Press.

———. 1991a. "Feminism and Vivisection." In *The Thee Generation: Reflections on the Coming Revolution*, 83–103. Philadelphia: Temple University Press.

———, ed. 1991b. *G. E. Moore: The Elements of Ethics*. Philadelphia: Temple University Press.

———. 1991c. "The Business of the Ethical Philosopher." In *Explorations of Value*, ed. Thomas Magnell, 93–104. Amsterdam and Atlanta: Rodopi. (Chapter 8 of the present volume.)

———. 2000. "Patterns of Resistance: The Struggle for Freedom and Equality in America." Unpublished paper. See chapter 6 of this volume.

Singer, Peter. 1975. *Animal Liberation*. New York: New York Review Books; dist. Random House.

Slicer, Deborah. 1991. "Your Daughter or Your Dog." *Hypatia* 6, no. 1:108–24.

Vance, Richard P. 1992. "An Introduction to the Philosophical Presuppositions of the Animal Liberation/Rights Movement." *Journal of the American Medical Association* 268:1715–19.

4

MAPPING HUMAN RIGHTS

In October 1997 Australia's University of Melbourne host-
ed an international, multidisciplinary conference entitled "Environmental
Justice: Global Ethics for the 21st Century." The participants represented
several disciplines, including economics, anthropology, architecture, history, and environmental science,as well as philosophy. In fact, the philosopher
Arne Naess was featured as the keynote speaker, and the plenary session in
which I was invited to participate included the philosophers Peter Singer
and Val Plumwood.

My contribution was crafted with a narrow focus. Those participating
in my session had been asked to consider whether it was possible for a human ethic to be "mapped on to the consideration of the human-nature relationship." The most I could do, I decided, was to explore several arguments that purport to show that such a mapping is not possible, at least in
the case of a rights-based human ethic. For reasons explained in the following discussion, the particular arguments I selected for examination are
ones favored by the philosopher Carl Cohen. Anyone who had come to
the conference expecting me to present some grand scheme of the moral
universe had to be more than a little disappointed when (or if) they read
the paper under my name in the passel of presentations distributed to at-
tendees.

Although the paper is limited in what it attempts to show and written in
the analytic style nonphilosophers seldom find magnetic, I think the matters I explore are important. Narrow they may be; still, I believe they help
chart the depth and breadth of the animal rights debate. Clearly, nonhuman
animals do not have rights if they cannot have them, and if they cannot have
them (that is, if their having rights is logically impossible), then advocates
of animal rights are confused at best and stupid at worst. Whether animals

can have rights is therefore something worthy of careful consideration. Because Cohen's challenge takes the form of denying the very possibility of animals' having rights, his supporting arguments, even if they are defective (as I believe them to be), deserve to be taken seriously rather than summarily dismissed.

"Mapping Human Rights" originally appeared in *Global Ethics*, ed. Nicholas Low, 158–74 (London: Routledge, 1999). Reprinted with the permission of the publisher.

❖

Philosophers have written more about animal rights in the past twenty years than their predecessors wrote in the previous two thousand. Not surprisingly, disagreements abound. To begin with, among those who challenge attributing moral rights to animals are philosophers who operate within well-worn moral traditions in Western thought. Peter Singer (1975, 1999) and Carl Cohen (1986, 1996, 1997) are representative. Singer follows in the tradition of the nineteenth-century English utilitarian Jeremy Bentham, who ridicules moral rights as "nonsense upon stilts." For both Bentham and Singer, not only nonhuman animals but also humans lack moral rights. This is half-true, maintains Cohen. Animals, he argues, most certainly do not have moral rights, but Bentham and Singer err when they deny that humans have them. Nothing could be further from the truth. According to Cohen, not just some but *all* humans possess basic rights, including the rights to life and to bodily integrity.

As different as Singer and Cohen are in the answers they give, they are importantly similar in the way they approach the question of animals rights in particular and the more fundamental question of moral right and wrong in general. Both operate in what might be described as the Enlightenment tradition. Both assume that moral right and wrong are matters that in principle can be determined by the disciplined use of reason, just as both assume that the answers we seek must pay proper deference to the privileged moral position of certain individuals—individual human beings in Cohen's case and individual sentient beings in Singer's.

Despite their many differences, Singer and Cohen occupy common ground with philosophical advocates of animal rights, a point easily lost in the storm of controversy (Pluhar 1995; Regan 1983; Rollin 1981; Sapontzis 1987). The latter also operate in the Enlightenment tradition; in other words, like Singer and Cohen, philosophical advocates of animal rights believe that moral right and wrong are matters that in principle can be determined by the disciplined use of reason and that the answers we seek must pay proper deference to the privileged position of certain individuals. Thus, Cohen's and Singer's quarrels with philosophical advocates of animal rights are of an "intramoral" nature. Even as they differ in the conclusions they reach, these philosophers all share a number of fundamental beliefs concerning what they do and how to do it.

Val Plumwood (1993, 1999) is representative of a different family of critics of animal rights. Like intramoral critics, Plumwood denies that animals have moral rights; unlike these critics, Plumwood also denies certain assumptions these critics share with philosophical advocates of animal rights. In particular, whereas both these advocates and their critics believe that answers to moral questions must pay proper deference to the privileged moral position of certain individuals, Plumwood believes that according a privileged moral position to a select group of individuals—for example, all human beings (Cohen's view) or all sentient beings (Singer's view)—is part of the problem, not part of the solution. What is needed, in her view, is a radical, nonhierarchical reconceptualization of the place of humans and other beings in the larger community of life. Because philosophical advocates of animal rights are committed to the privileged moral position of individual animals, these philosophies are an impediment to philosophical and indeed moral progress.

Criteria of Selection

The arguments against extending a rights-based human ethic to nonhuman animals are rich and varied, and nothing like a complete examination of these controversies can be attempted here. Let me explain my two reasons for examining those arguments I do.

First, as a matter of personal preference, I did not want to repeat any of my previously published responses to criticisms of animal rights—neither my responses to foundational critiques, including my replies to those philosophers, like Plumwood, who object to the Enlightenment prejudices allegedly embedded in the idea of the rights of the individual (Regan 1991), nor my responses to more specific criticisms of utilitarianism, including the form of utilitarianism favored by Singer (Regan 1980). Because I wanted to try to say something new (new for me, at least), I have nothing more to say on these matters here—and thus nothing further to say about the positions of Plumwood and Singer.

In addition to my personal interest in not repeating myself, my second interest is political in nature. I wanted to respond to those arguments that seem to be having the greatest influence among those who oppose the idea of animal rights in the larger world outside academic philosophy. Among the many possible candidates in this regard, Carl Cohen's criticisms of animal rights arguably satisfy this second basis of selection better than any other philosopher's. Since I have not commented on his ideas before and thus would not be repeating myself in responding to them, the following discussion examines Cohen's arguments against the possibility of extending a rights-based ethic to nonhuman animals.

A Question of the Logically Possible

We all are familiar with the idea that human beings have certain basic moral rights, including the rights to life, liberty, and bodily integrity. Some, like Cohen, think this familiar idea is true; others, including Singer and Plumwood, think it false. Just as there is plenty of room for disagreement among those who think the former (for example, concerning how the idea of a moral right should be understood), so there is plenty of room for disagreement among the latter.

Notwithstanding these differences, one way of understanding human ethics includes the attribution of basic moral rights to human beings, so if one were to attempt to show that no conception of human ethics can be "mapped on to the consideration of the human-nature relationship," one would be obliged to consider whether a rights-based human ethic, an ethic in which basic moral rights are attributed to human beings, can be "mapped" onto any aspect of the human-nature relationship, the human-animal relationship in particular. Moreover, in this latter regard, one would be obliged to examine arguments that attempt to show either that a rights-based human ethic cannot be extended to nonhuman animals (meaning that it is not even logically possible to do this) or that, while it might be logically possible to attempt such an extension, it should not be extended in this fashion.

In this chapter I explore only one of these options, limiting my remarks to arguments that purport to show that it is not logically possible to extend a rights-based human ethic to nonhuman animals. Thus, even if, against all the odds, it should happen that everything I say is correct, and every argument I formulate is valid, everyone should recognize that I would not have shown that such an ethic can or should be extended in the manner under review. Merely to show the inadequacy of some arguments against the possibility of this extension does not prove that such an extension is either possible or desirable.

Cohen's View

Of all those philosophers who have criticized the idea of animal rights, none has enjoyed greater influence than Cohen, especially among scientists who use nonhuman animals in their research. The genesis of this influence can be traced to a "special article" that appeared in the *New England Journal of Medicine* (Cohen 1986). For a philosopher to have his or her work appear as the lead article in such a prestigious nonphilosophical professional journal is no mean achievement; the pride of place accorded the essay reflects both the high regard in which Cohen is held by members of the biomedical research community and the perceived importance of the issues he examines.

In this article Cohen goes beyond offering a justification of using non-human animals in biomedical research. Not only is it not wrong to use animals for this purpose; Cohen argues that it would be wrong not to use them. For example, he writes: "If biomedical investigators abandon the effective pursuit of their professional objectives because they are convinced that they may not do to animals what the service of humans requires, they will fail, objectively, to do their duty" (Cohen 1986:868). Indeed, not only are researchers under a positive obligation to use them; Cohen argues that more rather than fewer animals should be used in certain circumstances. "Should we not at least reduce the use of animals in biomedical research?" Cohen asks, answering: "No, we should increase it, to avoid when feasible the use of humans as experimental subjects" (ibid.)

Cohen's reasoning in support of continued widespread and possibly expanded reliance on nonhuman animals in biomedical research is of the utilitarian variety. "The sum of the benefits [of using nonhuman animals in biomedical research] is utterly beyond quantification," Cohen writes. "Almost every new drug discovered, almost every disease eliminated, almost every vaccine developed, almost every method of pain relief devised, almost every surgical procedure invented, almost every prosthetic device implanted—indeed, almost every modern medical therapy is due, in part or in whole, to experimentation using animal subjects" (1986:868).

Along with acknowledging these benefits to humans, of course, utilitarians must also consider the harms done to nonhuman animals. "Let us do the weighing asked, by all means," Cohen insists, concluding:

The pain that is caused to humans (and to nonhuman animals) by diseases and disorders now curable, or one day very probably curable, through the use of laboratory animals, is so great as to be beyond calculation. What has already been accomplished is enough to establish that. What is now being accomplished, its benefits not yet in hand, would establish that truth with equal sureness even if only partially successful. And a fair weighing will put on the scales also those great medical achievements not yet even dreamed of but likely to be realized one day. (1996:9.39–40)*

"To refrain from using animals in biomedical research is, on utilitarian grounds, morally wrong" (Cohen 1986:868).

Although allowing that a small handful of researchers may on occasion be guilty of varying degrees of misconduct, Cohen assures his readers that the work carried out by biomedical researchers who use nonhuman animals is otherwise beyond moral reproach. Given his unqualified adulation of their work and his broad and deep justification of animal-model research, it is small wonder that many in the biomedical community see in Cohen their long awaited savior, sent to defend their good name and life-saving work against the abuse of such philosophical bullies as Peter Singer (1975), Bernard Rollin (1981), Steve Sapontzis (1987), and Evelyn Pluhar (1995).

Cohen has offered additional critiques of animal rights and presently has another in process (Cohen 1996). There is little to choose among these works, in my opinion, and I will treat them as together constituting what I call "Cohen's view." Although this view seeks to justify human use of other animals in biomedical research in particular, it rests on a critique of animal rights in general, including the rights of animals living in the wild ("in nature"). Given Cohen's position, it is just as logically impossible for nonhuman animals living in the natural world to have rights as it is for nonhuman animals living in a laboratory to have them. If correct, Cohen's view would thus entail that a particular conception of human ethics—the one where humans are represented as having basic moral rights—cannot be mapped onto the human-nature relationship.

Before turning to an examination of Cohen's critique, I want to summarize the broad contours of his view, first discussing how he understands moral rights and why he thinks this is an important idea.

---

* This work, an unpublished manuscript, consists of eleven short chapters, each chapter paginated separately; citations of quoted material indicate both chapter number and page number(s). I gratefully acknowledge Carl Cohen's permission to quote from this work-in-progress. For fuller elaborations of our respective views, see Tom Regan and Carl Cohen, *The Animals Rights Debate* (Lanham, Md.: Rowman and Littlefield, 2001).

The Importance of Animal Rights

"Rights trump interests" (Cohen 1996:4.3). Cohen makes this point not once but several times. His meaning is clear. Moral rights are like invisible moral No Trespassing signs. If I have a moral right to bodily integrity, for example, then you are not morally entitled to take one of my kidneys (to trespass my right) simply on the ground that you or someone else will benefit from having it. Similarly, if nonhuman animals have a right to bodily integrity, then humans are not morally entitled to take a kidney from a pig (to trespass the pig's right) simply on the ground that some human being will benefit from having the pig's kidney. Indeed, except in rare cases—for example, cases where it is necessary to hurt or kill an animal in self-defense—animals' having rights would undermine the morality of our hurting or killing them in the course of advancing any of our interests, even important interests such as health and life. As Cohen notes: "If animals have any rights at all they have the right to be respected, the right not to be used like a tool to advance human interests . . . no matter how important those human interests are thought to be" (1996:4.1). In other words, if nonhuman animals have rights, then research that utilizes them is wrong and should be stopped.

Cohen has good news for those scientists who use nonhuman animals in their research. These animals do not have rights. Indeed, they cannot have rights. The belief in animal rights he characterizes as a "fanatical conviction," "a profound and gigantic mistake" that is "ill-founded and dangerous" (1996:4.6, 1.8). Less dramatically, he calls the belief that rats have rights "silly" (5.4).

Of the many disparaging things Cohen says about the belief in animal rights, his characterization of it as "dangerous" merits further comment. Cohen claims that if the belief in animal rights were to prompt us to cease using nonhuman animals in research, humans, not to mention other animals, would pay a terrible price in terms of loss of benefits—benefits that, in his view, are "utterly beyond quantification." Without the freedom to use nonhuman animals for experimental purposes, Cohen believes, none or, at most, vastly fewer of these benefits would be possible. This consequence is what makes animal rights the "dangerous" idea it is, why steps must be taken to ensure that "research is not crippled by ignorant zealotry" (Cohen 1996:9.40), and why Cohen clearly sees his critique of this "fanatical conviction" as an important, honorable service to humanity.

Animal Psychology

Cohen does not make his task an easy one, as it would be if he had followed today's neo-Cartesians, such as Peter Carruthers (1992), by denying animals a mental life. To his credit, Cohen has a robust view of animal psychology, one that, in all essential respects, coincides both with the view I favor and with the settled convictions of all people of common sense. If for purposes of argument we simplify matters, applying the claims made about nonhuman animals only to mammals and birds, then we can say that Cohen believes these animals have cognitive, communicative, affective, and other noteworthy psychological capacities, including sentience. These animals can reason. They have an emotional life. They can plan and choose. Moreover, some things they experience give them pleasure, while others cause them pain. In these and other respects, these animals are like us, and we, like them.

Human Uniqueness and Rights

Still, there are important differences. In particular, Cohen believes that nonhuman animals are not morally responsible for their actions. Whatever they do, it is not and indeed cannot be morally right; by the same token, it neither is nor can be morally wrong. Like the ideas of moral right and wrong, moral responsibility applies to humans and—at least among terrestrial forms of life—to humans only.

While Cohen has no doubt that humans have rights (humans "certainly have rights," he insists at one point [1996:5.1]), he never defends this point. What he does instead is clarify this (in his words) "central moral question of all time" by summarizing some of "the *kinds* of explanations of human rights that have been given by the greatest moral philosophers" (5.11). Cohen's list is eclectic, including explanations by philosophers as diverse as St. Thomas Aquinas, F. H. Bradley, John Dewey, and Karl Marx, philosophers who, despite their obvious differences, Cohen says agree with him in thinking that there is something uniquely important about being human. "Moral philosophers through the ages," Cohen writes, "have not disagreed about *the essentially human locus of the concept of right.* Of the finest thinkers from antiquity to the present not one would deny—as the animal rights movement does seek to deny—that there is a fundamental difference between the moral stature of humans and that of animals" (5.11).

When it comes to specifying this "fundamental difference," Cohen displays a certain fondness for Kant's views. He sides with Kant in extolling the "unique capacity of humans to formulate moral *principles* for the direction of our conduct, to grasp the maxim of the principles we devise, and by applying these principles to ourselves as well as to others, to exhibit the moral *autonomy* of the human will." (1996:4.12). Nonhuman animals, on both Kant's and Cohen's view, lack these capacities. On this point Kant and Cohen certainly seem to be correct. Even philosophers such as Sapontzis, who discerns the workings of a proto-morality in the loyal, courageous, and empathetic behavior of nonhuman animals, stop short of supposing that wolves and elephants trouble themselves over deciding whether the maxims of their actions can be willed to be universal laws.

In general, then, Cohen believes—and with all this I agree—that humans and other animals resemble each other in many ways and differ in others. Like us, other animals have a complicated, unified psychology involving cognitive, affective, volitional, and other capacities. Unlike humans, however, other animals lack the sophisticated abilities that make moral autonomy, agency, and responsibility possible. In this respect humans are unique, at least among terrestrial creatures. So far, so good.

Duties to Animals

Cohen thinks we have duties to animals, not merely duties involving them. "We humans have, and recognize that we have, many *obligations* to animals," he writes (Cohen 1996:5.1). In particular, "the obligation to act humanely *we owe to them*" (5.4). Mammals (at least) are "morally considerable," and "we humans surely ought cause no pain to them that cannot be justified. Nor ought we to kill them without reason" (5.8). Again, "we are obliged to apply to animals the moral principles that govern *us* regarding the gratuitous imposition of pain and suffering" (5.4).

Fairly clearly, then, Cohen regards his position as what I have called a direct, rather than indirect, duty view (see chapter 1 of the present volume). Those who hold some version of the latter type (an indirect duty view) believe that although we can have duties involving nonhuman animals, we have no duties to them. For example, if your neighbor mistreats your dog, you will be upset. It is because it is wrong to upset you, not because of any wrong done to your dog, that an indirect duty theorist might say that your neighbor has failed to do his duty with respect to your dog. On such a view, dogs and other nonhuman animals have the same moral standing, the same moral considerability, as sticks and stones. When assessed from the moral point of view, other-than-human animals, like sticks and stones, themselves count for nothing.

To Cohen's credit, he does not wish to align himself with such indirect duty theorists as the early twentieth-century Jesuit Joseph Rickaby, whose views are representative of the type. Writes Rickaby: "We have . . . no duties . . . of any kind, to . . . animals, as neither to sticks and stones" (1976:179). Not true, according to Cohen. If your neighbor mistreats your dog, Cohen would insist that your neighbor *has done something wrong to the dog*. On this point, as on many others, Cohen certainly seems to be on the side of the angels. To support this judgment, consider the following two cases.

First, suppose your neighbor breaks your leg for no good reason. No one will deny that this hurts—a lot. Similarly beyond question is that your neighbor has harmed you directly. Of course, others might be upset or even outraged that you have been so badly mistreated. But even if no one is upset—even if everyone else in the neighborhood is positively delighted about your misfortune—there is no question that *you* have been harmed, that *you* have suffered a serious wrong.

Next, suppose your neighbor does the same thing, only this time it is your dog whose leg is broken for no good reason. Well, that hurts your dog—a lot. Moreover, your neighbor has harmed your dog directly. How can all this be true and yet it also be true that in breaking your leg, your neighbor *has* done a direct wrong to you, but in breaking your dog's leg, your neighbor *has not* done a direct wrong to your dog? As far as I can see, the two cases are the same in all the morally relevant respects. Thus, short of following the neo-Cartesians by denying that nonhuman animals feel pain, I do not see how it can be true that your neighbor has a direct duty to you not to cause you pain and harm for no good reason but has no parallel direct duty to your dog. If I am right about this, then to be credible, Cohen will have to agree that at least some of our duties are duties owed directly to such animals.

As was previously mentioned, Cohen believes all this. I do not see how his claims about our moral ties to other animals permit any other interpretation. For reasons given later, however, he cannot consistently hold this position. As I hope to show, if Cohen's arguments against animals' having rights were successful, these same arguments would also show, mutatis mutandis, that we have no duties to them.

Before explaining the dilemma Cohen faces, I need to say something further by way of a general characterization of his view, particularly his understanding of the relationship between rights and duties.

Duties and Rights

From the presumed fact that we have duties directly to animals, Cohen argues that it does not follow that they have rights against us. This certainly seems to be correct. In the case of the moral ties that bind humans to one another, there are many cases where our duties do not have correlative rights. For example, I have a duty to render assistance to those in need, but no particular needy person has a right to demand that I discharge this duty by assisting her or him. Moreover, even when the duty is owed to a specific individual (for example, someone who has been especially kind or thoughtful), there need be no correlative right. "A special act of kindness done to us," Cohen notes, "may leave us with the obligation to acknowledge and return that kindness—but the benefactor to whom we are obligated has no claim of *right* against us" (1996:5.3).

It would therefore be a mistake, as Cohen is correct to see, to infer that animals have rights simply because we have direct duties to them, whether to all animals or only to specific ones. Although it is true that all rights have correlative duties, it is false that all duties have correlative rights, let alone that all duties "arise from rights" (Cohen 1996:5.2). On this point, Cohen will get no argument from me.

The problem is that he will get no argument from anyone—at least not anyone of whom I am aware, including in particular those (less than the "greatest") philosophers who maintain that animals have rights or that humans and other animals share an equal moral status. Even a position like mine, where duties are treated as the basis of rights, need not claim that rights are correlated with or arise from each and every duty. In my view (Regan 1983), it is only when duties are basic and unacquired—only in the case of duties such as the duty of justice, for example, as distinct from those duties we have to our employers—that we may validly infer correlative rights. Possibly I am mistaken about this. I would certainly be obliged to consider carefully any argument that purported to show that I am. Since Cohen's argument fails to address my views, however, there is nothing to consider. One does not show that no duties have correlative rights simply by showing that some duties do not have correlative rights.

The Amorality Rights Argument

How, then, does Cohen attempt to prove that animals do not and cannot have rights? Although he does not clearly distinguish them, I think Cohen relies on at least three different arguments; and while all three are related to one another, each differs in important ways from the other two. The first argument grows from Cohen's claim that animals are *amoral*. This is an idea he introduces after asking us to imagine a lioness who kills a baby zebra. He writes:

> Do you believe the baby zebra has the *right* not to be slaughtered by that lioness? Does that lioness have the *right* to kill that baby zebra for her cubs? If you are inclined to say, confronted by such natural rapacity— duplicated a thousand, a million times each day on planet earth—that neither is right or wrong, and that neither has a *right* against the other, I am on your side. Rights are of the highest moral consequence, yes; but zebras and lions and rats are *a*moral; there is no morality for them; they do no wrong, ever. In their world there are no rights. (Cohen 1997:95)

Essentially, then, what we have is the following:

The Amorality Rights Argument
1. Animals live in an amoral world (a world where nothing is right or wrong).
2. Those who live in an amoral world have no rights.
3. Therefore, animals have no rights.

Sapontzis's reservations about the moral agency of animals notwithstanding, suppose we agree that animals are incapable of doing what is right and wrong. Concerning their interactions with one another, let us agree that it makes no sense to say that the baby zebra has a right not to be killed by the lioness or that the lioness has a duty not to kill the baby zebra. From this Cohen would have us infer that it makes no sense to say that the baby zebra (or any other animal, for that matter) has a right against us—for example, the right not to be killed by us for no good reason. Not only does this not follow; it is inconsistent with Cohen's claims about our duties to animals.

To make this clearer, consider a parallel argument that concerns duties, not rights.

The Amorality Duties Argument
1. Animals live in an amoral world (a world where nothing is right or wrong).
2. Those who live in an amoral world have no duties.
3. Therefore, animals have no duties.

Cohen unquestionably accepts this argument's conclusion. As was previously shown, however, to be credible, Cohen must believe that *we* have direct duties to animals; indeed, he accepts this view. For Cohen, then, the claim that nonhuman animals have no duties to one another is and must be perfectly consistent with our having duties to them.

Logically, the possibility of nonhuman animals' having rights is no different. From the presumed fact that animals do not have rights against one another, it does not follow that they do not, let alone that they cannot, have rights against us. Possibly they do not. Possibly they cannot. Nevertheless, whether they do or do not, can or cannot, is not something that can be settled by insisting that their world contains no right or wrong, no duty, no respect for or violation of the moral rights of others.

It bears noting that the logical point at issue here is independent of determining whether duties and rights are correlative. Suppose for the sake of argument that duties and rights never are correlative—that, in other words, one can never validly infer duties from rights, or vice versa. That would not affect the present criticism. The present criticism insists only that one cannot validly infer that (a) animals cannot have rights against us because (b) they do not or cannot have rights against one another, any more than one can validly infer that (c) we cannot have duties to them because (d) they do not or cannot have duties to one another. In other words, the criticism concerns what follows from animals' not having duties or rights, not what follows from someone's having a duty or someone's having a right, and is thus quite independent of the relation between rights and duties.

The Right-Kind Argument

Cohen has a second argument that stands or falls independently of the first. This one concerns "the capacity for moral judgment." If nonhuman animals are denied rights because they are unable to exercise this capacity, why is not the same thing true of "many humans—the brain-damaged, the comatose, the senile?" Cohen replies as follows.

> This objection fails; it mistakenly treats an essential feature of humanity as though it were a screen for sorting humans. The capacity for moral judgment that distinguishes humans from animals is not a test to be administered to human beings one by one. Persons who are unable, because of some disability, to perform the full moral functions natural to human beings are certainly not for that reason ejected from the mor-

al community. The issue is one of kind. Humans are of a kind that they may be the subject of experiments only with their voluntary consent. The choices they make freely must be respected. Animals are of such a kind that it is impossible for them, in principle, to give or withhold voluntary consent or to make a moral choice. What humans retain when disabled, animals have never had. (Cohen 1986:866)

Cohen's meaning is not admirably clear, partly because it is not clear what disabled humans "retain." Certainly it cannot be the capacities in question, since it is their lack of these very capacities that helps define their disabilities, and it makes no sense to say they retain what they lack.

What, then, do they retain? Well, presumably they retain their rights. If we ask why, Cohen's answer turns on considerations about what kind of being human beings are. In his view, possession of the capacities that make rights possible (for example, the capacity of moral judgment) defines the kind of being humans are. Nonhuman animals lack these capacities. Whereas such a lack is a defect for a human being, it is nothing of the sort for other animals. Nonhuman animals simply are not the right kind of being to have rights; human beings—and all and only human beings—are. Thus we have Cohen's second argument.

The Right-Kind Argument

1. Individuals have rights if and only if they are the right kind of being.
2. All and only humans are the right kind of being (that is, have the capacities that make possession of rights possible).
3. Therefore, all and only humans have rights.

This argument is strongly counterintuitive. If moral rights are rights *possessed by individuals*, by what manner or means can we fairly decide which individuals have them without resting our decision on the morally relevant capacities different individuals possess? Imagine that a university annually awards a scholarship in mathematics. Will anyone suggest that we may fairly decide who deserves it without bothering to ask about the mathematical abilities of the several candidates, considered individually? Why should our judgment concerning which individuals possess rights be any different?

To make my misgivings plainer, consider the following *Gedanken* experiment. Imagine that a party of extraterrestrials (let us suppose it is E.T. and his friends) make contact with us humans. They give every indication of possessing those capacities Cohen believes are essential features of being human. Suppose further that the capacities they share are not essential, not typical of the species to which they belong. E.T. and his cohort are genetic aberrations, cruising the universe in search of others of their kind.

Given Cohen's view, these extraterrestrials lack rights. Indeed, they cannot possibly have them. Why? Because those capacities they possess, as the individuals they are, are not essential to the kind of being they happen to be. "Sorry, E.T.," we will have to say, "but you and your friends do not have any rights."

"But why?" E.T. asks. "We have all the capacities you humans have."

"Yes," we reply, "but we have them because they are essential to the kind of being we are, while your having them is some sort of genetic accident."

On any credible account of rights, E.T. and his cohort have them not because (or only if) they are of the "right kind" but because they as individuals have rights-conferring capacities. In this sense, contrary to Cohen, relevant criteria for possessing rights *do* serve as "a screen for sorting," not for humans only, but for all would-be candidates. It is for this reason that, Cohen's right-kind argument notwithstanding, the question whether any nonhuman animals qualify remains open.

The Community Argument

Cohen has a third argument against the possibility of animals' having rights. Unlike the amorality rights argument, which builds on the allegedly amoral condition of nonhuman animals, and unlike the right-kind argument, which rests on allegedly essential features of kinds of beings, this third argument is grounded in the way rights arise among those who have them. "Rights," Cohen declares, "are universally human; they arise in a *human moral world*, in a moral *sphere*. In the world of humankind moral judgments are pervasive, and it is the fact that all humans, including infants and the senile, are members of that community—not the fact that as individuals they have or do not have certain special capacities, or properties—that makes humans bearers of rights" (1996:5.14).

Other animals, alas, are not members of (this) community and so lack rights, whatever their capacities might be. Bring forth whatever impressive list of capacities and achievements in the case of any nonhuman animal one might wish (communicative skills among nonhuman primates, the cleverness of cats, the sagacity of wolves) and compare these animals with a human bereft of all cognitive and volitional abilities; it matters not. The human has rights, and the other animals do not.

It is beside the point to insist that animals have remarkable capacities, that they really have a consciousness of self, or of the future, or make plans, and so on. And the tired response that because infants plainly cannot make moral claims they must have no rights at all, or that rats must have them too, we ought forever put aside. Responses like these arise out of a misconception of right itself. They mistakenly suppose that rights are tied to some identifiable individual capacities, or sensibilities, and they fail to see that rights arise only in a community of moral beings, and that therefore there are spheres in which rights do apply and spheres in which they do not. (Cohen 1997:94–95)

I think any honest reading of this passage will have to conclude that Cohen's meaning is not as clear as one might wish. Let me try to explain what I think he means; then I will be able to explain why I believe he is mistaken.

Cohen states that rights "arise" in a "human moral world," "in a moral sphere," in a "community" (meaning, presumably, a "moral community"). I take Cohen to mean that the very idea of a moral right assumes a social context without which this idea could not arise. Cohen and I agree that rights place justified limits on the ways in which individuals may be treated; for example, we agree that our right to life entails that others are not at liberty to kill us except in unusual circumstances (in self-defense, say). That being so, the idea of rights can arise only if (a) individuals are living together and interacting with one another, and (b) these individuals can understand what it means to have justified limitations on what they are free to do to one another. Human beings, Cohen thinks, satisfy both these conditions. Arguably, no other animals do.

True, nonhuman animals who live in groups in the wild satisfy condition a, but it is implausible in the extreme to maintain that they also satisfy condition b. Granted, *we* may be able to limit their liberty, but it is pure fancy, I think, to imagine that members of a wolf pack, for example, can understand the idea of deliberately imposing justifiable limits on their behavior. This is why zebras and gazelles, for example, cannot understand what a right is and why rights cannot arise in a community of these animals.

The same is no less true of those animals who live in community with us. For example, Professor Cohen shares his life with a beloved son and a dog. And there can be no doubt that both father and son lavish their love and affection on this lucky animal. But while it is true that the dog is a member of the "Cohen community" in one sense, this is not the sense in which the human members of the Cohen family belong to the human *moral* community. For the Cohen dog, like every other dog that has existed, currently is alive, or will one day roam the earth, never has understood, does not now understand, and never will understand that moral rights place justified limits on the acts individuals are free to do. This being so, the idea of rights can arise no more among domesticated animals than among wild ones.

What of those human beings (including, for example, infants, the insane, and the seriously mentally disadvantaged) who, like both wild and domesticated animals, are unable to understand what moral rights are? Granted, these humans are members of the human community, not in some extended sense (as when we say, for example, that the Cohens' dog is an "honorary" member of the Cohen family), but literally: they all *are* human beings. Like the "honorary" canine member of the Cohen family, however, these humans do not now understand what a right is, and many of them never will. Do these humans have rights?

Again, Cohen says they do. He believes that although the inability of animals to understand what rights are is sufficient to exclude them from the class of right-holders, this same lack of understanding does not disqualify any human being. Every human being has rights because all are members of the community in which the idea of rights arises, whereas every nonhuman animal lacks rights because none belongs to this community. Clearly, then, the decisive criterion for possessing rights is not whether one understands what rights are; it is whether one is a member of the community in which rights arise. Since the only community in which rights arise, at least in the terrestrial sphere, is the community composed of human beings, in that sphere being a human (belonging to the species *Homo sapiens*) is both a necessary and sufficient condition of possessing rights.

I believe the foregoing captures both what Cohen believes and why he believes it. Let me summarize his argument as follows.

The Community Argument

1. All and only those individuals have rights who are members of communities in which the idea of rights arises.
2. Within the terrestrial sphere, the idea of rights arises only in the human community.
3. Therefore, within that sphere, all and only humans have rights.

It should be fairly obvious why and how this argument goes wrong. Conceptually, there is a distinction between (a) the necessary and sufficient conditions of the origin or formation of an idea and (b) the scope of the idea. The former concerns how it is possible for an idea (to use Cohen's word) to "arise," whereas the latter concerns the range of objects or individuals to which or to whom the idea may be intelligibly applied. The central point to recognize is that these two matters are logically separate in this sense: the scope of an idea is something that must be determined independently of considerations about its origins.

Consider the following example. As far as we know, ideas such as those of the notions of the central nervous system and genes are ideas that arise only among humans because only humans have the requisite cognitive capacities to form them. Nonetheless, the range of entities to which these ideas apply is not necessarily limited to members of the community in which these ideas arise. Indeed, not only is the scope of these ideas not necessarily limited to humans, but there are literally billions and billions of nonhuman animals to whom the ideas are correctly applied—who have, that is, genes and a central nervous system.

Rights are conceptually no different. I grant that, as far as we know, the idea of rights arises only among humans because only humans have the requisite cognitive capacities to understand it. Nevertheless, the range of entities to which this idea applies is not necessarily limited to members of the community in which the idea arises. Logically, to make this inference would be to make the same mistake made by one who infers that wolves cannot have genes or that the Cohens' dog cannot have a central nervous system because these animals do not belong to a community in which these ideas arise.

Conclusion

Among those philosophers critical of animal rights, none has commanded a larger audience outside philosophy or exercised a greater influence than Carl Cohen. Although I do not question the sincerity of his beliefs concerning animal rights, it has been my object here to show how ill supported those beliefs are. His central arguments (the amorality rights argument, the right-kind argument, and the community argument) are deeply, seriously, and, in my opinion, irredeemably flawed.

Of course, recognizing how and why Cohen's arguments go wrong does not prove that animals have rights, any more than we can prove which animals have a central nervous system just by recognizing that the scope of this idea is not necessarily limited to individuals who belong to a community in which this idea arises. Proving that animals have rights has not been the purpose of the present argument, however; if it had been, I would have been obliged to consider objections to this idea raised not only by Cohen but also by Peter Singer and Val Plumwood—to mention only two of the many other critics lined up against attributing rights to nonhuman animals. As I have been at pains to explain, my purpose on this occasion has been much more modest, limited to showing why Carl Cohen's arguments fail to prove that other-than-human animals cannot have rights. That much granted, I conclude that Cohen has failed to show that a familiar conception of human ethics—the one where humans are represented as possessing basic moral rights—cannot be "mapped on to the consideration of the human-nature relationship" in general, the human-nonhuman animal relationship in particular. My own positive account of one way in which this mapping can be done may be found elsewhere (Regan 1983).

Works Cited

Carruthers, Peter. 1992. *The Animal Issue*. Cambridge: Cambridge University Press.
Cohen, Carl. 1986. "The Case for the Use of Animals in Biomedical Research." *New England Journal of Medicine* 315, no. 14 (Oct. 2): 865–70.
———. 1996. "In Defense of the Use of Animals." Unpublished manuscript.
———. 1997. "Do Animals Have Rights?" *Ethics and Behavior* 7, no. 2:91–102.
Pluhar, Evelyn. 1995. *Beyond Prejudice: The Moral Significance of Human and Nonhuman Animals*. Durham, N.C.: Duke University Press.
Plumwood, Val. 1993. *Feminism and the Mastery of Nature*. London: Routledge.
———. 1999. "From Rights to Recognition: Eco-justice and Non-humans." In *Global Ethics*, ed. Nicholas Low, 88–212. London: Routledge.
Rickaby, Fr. Joseph. 1976. "Of the So-called Rights of Animals." In *Animal Rights and Human Obligations*, ed. Tom Regan and Peter Singer, 79–80. Englewood Cliffs, N.J.: Prentice-Hall.
Regan, Tom. 1980. "Utilitarianism, Vegetarianism, and Animal Rights." *Philosophy and Public Affairs* 9, no. 4:305–24; repr., Tom Regan, *All That Dwell Therein: Essays on Animal Rights and Environmental Ethics*, 40–60. Berkeley: University of California Press, 1982.
———. 1983. *The Case for Animal Rights*. Berkeley: University of California Press.
———. 1991. "Feminism and Vivisection." In *The Thee Generation: Reflections on the Coming Revolution*, 83–103. Philadelphia: Temple University Press.
Rollin, Bernard. 1981. *Animal Rights and Human Morality*. Buffalo, N.Y.: Prometheus Books.
Sapontzis, Steven. 1987. *Morals, Reason, and Animals*. Philadelphia: Temple University Press.
Singer, Peter. 1975. *Animal Liberation*. New York: Avon Books.
———. 1999. "Ethics across the Species Boundary." In *Global Ethics*, ed. Nicholas Low, 146–57. London: Routledge.

5

PUTTING PEOPLE IN THEIR PLACE

In May 1998 Gerhold Becker, the director of Hong Kong Baptist University's Centre for Applied Ethics, organized an international, multicultural symposium entitled "Bioethics and the Concept of Personhood." The occasion was as intellectually expanding as it was rewarding. Of particular interest were differences between the Western and the Chinese concepts of personhood. In Chinese thought the idea of personhood is logically and semantically wedded to the idea of human being, whereas in Western thought and language there is nothing conceptually or linguistically untoward in thinking or speaking of beings (for example, gods, angels, or extraterrestrials) who, while not human, are persons.

Whatever the extension of the concept of personhood, and however much this might vary from one culture to another, it has long seemed to me that far too much moral importance is attached to being a person. This is what I attempted to explain in my contribution to the symposium. That someone is a person is morally relevant, certainly, but that being a person makes one morally superior or confers on that individual moral rights no other living being can possibly possess—these claims seem to me to be more in the nature of arrogant dogma than reasoned belief.

In making this judgment, I join a number of other philosophers, including some of those whose work is cited along the way. To the best of my knowledge, however, the arguments I advance in support of this judgment are novel. Moreover, while my position has important implications regarding the moral status of nonhuman animals, it also has no less important implications concerning the moral status of many human beings, including young children and the mentally disadvantaged of all ages. In this respect, the conclusions I reach here are of a piece with those I have been attempting to support for more than twenty years. There is, I believe, nothing in the least bit misanthropic in advocating animal rights; on the contrary, the philosophical considerations that ground the rights of nonhuman animals are the same considerations that most adequately ground the rights of human beings, the most vulnerable among us in particular. I hope this chapter goes some small way toward making this judgment both clearer and more compelling.

"Putting People in Their Place" was initially published as "Poniendo a las personas en su sitio," *Teorema* 18, no. 3 (Sept. 1999): 17–38.

Many if not most contemporary Western moral philosophers accept the following three propositions.

1. Compared with everyone and everything else, persons have a unique, superior moral status.
2. All persons, and only persons, can have rights.
3. All persons, and only persons, do have rights.

For reasons I advance later, I believe that each of these widely shared beliefs is false. While it is true that, given certain conceptions, persons are unique in important ways, I argue that these are not ways that make them morally superior. Moreover, although it may be true that all persons can (or even do) possess rights, I argue that individuals who are not persons have rights if (as I shall assume) persons do.

I reach the conclusions I do by exploring two ways to approach the question, "Who has rights?" Both approaches sketched here leave major foundational questions unanswered; even so, I argue that one of the approaches is more plausible than the other. Because the more plausible approach implies that other-than-human animals have rights if persons do, the conclusions I reach should be of interest both to those scientists who use these animals in their research and to those members of the general public who support their doing so.

Rights

The domain of rights is rife with distinctions. My hope is to make things as simple as my limited objectives permit. In addition to distinguishing between moral and legal rights, it is commonplace to distinguish between positive rights (rights to be helped or assisted) and negative rights (rights not to be harmed or interfered with). My remarks throughout are confined to negative moral rights (hereafter "rights"), including the rights to life, to bodily integrity, and to liberty.

Rights share a number of important features; one in particular merits our attention. The feature I have in mind concerns how violating rights is tied to doing what is wrong. What I call "the moral tie" can be formulated as follows.

The moral tie: It is morally wrong routinely to override the rights of some individuals merely on the ground that others will benefit.

A moment's reflection confirms that the moral tie is not meant to be a definition of "morally wrong." After all, there are many ways to do what is morally wrong other than routinely overriding the rights of some so that others will benefit. Moreover, rights can be overridden and wrongs done in cases where the moral tie does not apply. For example, individuals who are permanently scarred as a result of a violent attack have their right to bodily integrity violated even if this is the only time such an attack occurs.

How, then, should the moral tie be understood? Its status, by my lights, is that of a general moral principle—general in that it applies to all actions of a certain type, and moral because it judges each action of this type to be morally wrong. Is this a plausible moral principle? I think so. The moral tie expresses a widely shared conviction about the way violations of moral rights are tied to commissions of moral wrongs. For example, most people would condemn institutionalized policies that routinely override the rights of some (for example, those judged "inferior" because of their race) merely because of the benefits others derive. Those of us who would issue this condemnation, however, would surely agree that such routine violation of individual rights is not wrong only when based on racial prejudice. *Whatever* the arbitrary basis, whether it be race, gender, ethnicity, or some other equally irrelevant characteristic, it is wrong routinely to override the rights of some merely so that others will benefit. As such, our condemnation of racist and other prejudicial practices can be viewed as special instances of the application of the moral tie.

The moral tie helps explain why rights have the special status they do. When we attribute rights to others, we mean to assert that treating them respectfully is more important than supporting policies that advance the good of others, including the good of society as a whole. To use Ronald Dworkin's famous analogy, we mean to assert that the rights of the individual "trump" even the best-intentioned practices designed to promote the general welfare (Dworkin 1977). Rights confer on their possessors a unique, privileged position in the "moral game." This is one reason individual rights are so important and the very idea of such rights is so controversial.

The moral tie does not preclude circumstances in which the rights of an individual may be justifiably overridden. After all, we live in an imperfect world—a world lacking a preestablished harmony that guarantees that rights of different individuals never come into conflict with one another. For example, imagine that two people carry a highly contagious, fatal disease. To protect others, the two must be quarantined, something they vigorously resist. Having no other realistic alternative, we decide to detain them involuntarily. Here, it seems, we have an instance where the liberty rights of two people are justifiably overridden, an instance, moreover, in which others benefit, at least in the sense that they are spared risk of serious harm. If this is true, should we conclude that the moral tie is false?

I do not think so. Notice, first, that like other, similar cases, this case does not contradict either the spirit or the letter of the moral tie. Recall that the moral tie states that it is wrong *routinely* to override someone's rights merely on the ground that others will benefit. The involuntary-detention and similar examples are importantly different. In such cases, we are not being asked to imagine that a particular individual's rights are routinely overridden. On the contrary, such cases are provocative precisely because they present exceptional circumstances. Rights need not be absolute (that is, permitting of no possible exceptions) to be rights. Nonetheless, to allow that there are exceptional situations in which the rights of some may be justifiably overridden because others will benefit does not mean (and does not commit one to the view) that rights justifiably may be routinely overridden merely on this ground. Indeed, given the "trump" feature of rights, to permit practices that routinely override individual rights merely because others will benefit is tantamount to denying that individuals have rights at all. Because the involuntary-detention and similar examples do not constitute cases where the rights of some are routinely overridden merely so that others will benefit, such cases do not represent counterinstances to the moral tie.

Note also that even when others benefit in cases where rights are justifiably overridden, it does not follow that the benefits others obtain are what justify overriding them. An alternative account of resolving conflicts of rights dispenses altogether with appeals to the benefits others derive. On this analysis, developed at length in *The Case for Animal Rights* (Regan 1983), our justification in overriding the rights of the infected people depends on the number of individuals whose rights are at stake, not on the amount that different individuals will benefit. Other things being equal, in cases of conflict, it is better to override the rights of the few rather than the rights of the many; in the present case, therefore, it is better to limit the liberty of the two contagious people than to expose countless numbers of people to the preventable risk of serious harm. Thus, on this analysis, the benefit that these latter individuals receive turns out to be a side effect of justifiably overriding the liberty rights of the two unfortunate people who carry the lethal disease, not the basis for justifiably overriding their rights in the first place.

I will not attempt to defend this approach to resolving conflicts of rights, contenting myself here with stating its broad outlines and referring interested readers to the developed statement found in the book to which I referred earlier. In any event, the substantive issues I want to raise can be highlighted even if it is true, as many proponents of rights believe, that we are sometimes justified in overriding the rights of some individuals merely so that others will benefit.

To proceed, I need to say something about the idea of doing something merely so that others will benefit. Not surprisingly, this idea is likely to resist a correct and exhaustive analysis. For starters, the notion of a benefit admits of any number of possible interpretations, as does the concept of others (one, a few, many, most?). Again, I have explored these ideas at length elsewhere (Regan 1983) and will not explore them further here.

What I do want to explore, albeit incompletely, is the meaning of *merely* in "merely so that others will benefit." I note, first, that, in one sense, *merely* does not mean "only" or "exclusively." Individuals can have their rights routinely overridden for many reasons besides the benefits others will derive from doing so. For example, the A's might routinely override the rights of the B's because the former believe they have been commanded by God to do so. Moreover, even when the benefits others derive *are* considered, they need not be the only consideration. For example, routinely overriding the rights of the B's might be a tradition among the A's, and the A's might think it important to honor their ancestors by practicing the traditions that have been handed down to them. The *merely* in "merely so that others will benefit," then, does not specify a necessary condition for the wrongness of overriding individual rights, and neither does it specify the only type of consideration that would make it wrong routinely to do so.

What *merely* does specify, I think, is a sufficient condition of wrongdoing, in this sense: if the benefits others derive are deemed to be *reason enough* for routinely overriding individual rights, then that in turn is reason enough to make a judgment of wrongdoing. For example, imagine that routinely overriding the rights of the B's is a well-entrenched tradition among the A's. Imagine, further, that the A's become convinced that behavior is not shown to be right just because it is a matter of tradition. That is, they are willing to set aside appeal to tradition as a basis for justifying the behavior in question—but not the benefits they derive from engaging in it. From their point of view, the benefits are reason enough routinely to override the rights of the B's, which in turn is reason enough, given the moral tie, to judge their behavior wrong.

Those of us who agree on the moral status of rights can disagree over who does (and who can) have them, and even over how we should decide this matter. Concerning this latter source of controversy, we can distinguish between two approaches. One (the "moral approach") seeks to determine who has rights by relying on moral judgments; the second (the "factual approach") relies on claims made about various empirical characteristics taken to be constitutive of personhood. I am uncertain whether any philosopher has deployed either of the two approaches exactly as I describe them. I am reasonably certain, however, that some of what I say resembles some things other philosophers have said about the matters at hand. Moreover, I make no pretense to completeness; clearly, there are other ways to approach the issues under review (for example, by relying on one or another version of contractarianism) that differ in important ways from the two I sketch. My intention is not to exhaust possible approaches or to provide detailed accounts of the positions favored by others; it is to describe two possible ways of approaching the question, "Who has rights?"

Rights: The Moral Approach

As the name suggests, the moral approach would have us determine which individuals have rights on the basis of moral judgments. Which moral judgments? Well, those that reflect the moral logic of the moral tie. Here, more specifically, is what I mean.

The moral tie states that treating certain individuals (those who have rights) in certain ways (for example, routinely overriding their rights by taking their lives or disfiguring their bodies) is wrong when such treatment is done merely so that others will benefit. In other words, routinely overriding individual rights for that reason is a sufficient condition of wrongdoing. That being so, one way to approach the question about the bearers of rights is to ask the following question:

For any group of individuals (the A's), would it be wrong routinely to harm them (for example, by killing them or disfiguring their bodies) merely so that others will benefit?

If the answer is yes, then the moral approach implies that the A's have rights, because the wrongness of how the A's are treated exemplifies the wrongness of how rights-bearers are treated. In both cases (that is, both in the case of acknowledged rights-bearers and in the case of the A's), it is wrong routinely to harm them merely so that others will benefit. What the moral approach proposes, then, is that an affirmative answer to the question posed constitutes at least a sufficient basis for the attribution of rights (I leave open whether it is also necessary).

The moral approach has certain advantages. For example, it provides a basis for saying (and explicating) why strapping teenagers and their middle-aged parents possess rights, regardless of race, ethnicity, class, or sexual orientation. That basis is grounded in (1) morality and (2) what I have termed the moral logic of the moral tie. It is because it is wrong routinely to harm strapping teenagers and their middle-aged parents merely so that others will benefit that both the parents and their children have rights.

All is not clear sailing for the moral approach. For one thing, people often differ over the moral judgments they make. Because (given this approach) "the moral" determines who has rights, the moral approach by its very nature must describe and justify a method for determining which moral judgments are well grounded or true. As sketched here, the moral approach manifestly fails to do this. Worse, it is possible that no moral judgments are valid or well grounded; for example, it is possible that all are purely emotive in their meaning, in which case the idea of the rights of the individual would be more in the nature of wish fulfillment than moral fact. Unless or until these foundational metaethical challenges are met, the moral approach fails to provide a definitive justification for ascribing rights to anyone.

Rights: The Factual Approach

The factual approach regarding rights possession denies the priority of the moral. The approach favored here is to specify a set of nonmoral, empirically verifiable characteristics deemed to be constitutive of personhood. Different philosophers cite different characteristics. Some favor a small handful of characteristics—for example, rationality and autonomy. Others prefer a larger inventory, including (in addition to rationality and autonomy) all or some of the following: consciousness, self-awareness (understood as the capacity to project one's existence into the future), sentience, and the abilities to communicate, feel emotions, and act intentionally. Whatever set of characteristics is preferred, those individuals who possess the defining characteristics are deemed to be persons, whereas those individuals who lack these characteristics, whatever else might be true of them, are classified as nonpersons. Of the various ways to think about the nature of personhood from a factual perspective, the idea that all and only persons are both rational and autonomous appears to be the most widely accepted, and unless otherwise indicated, my following remarks are limited to this conception.

The factual approach resonates with the widely shared belief in the unique, superior moral status of persons. Because persons (and only persons) are rational and autonomous, it is argued that persons (and only persons) have the status of morally responsible agents. Given certain conceptions of moral agency, this proposal seems eminently reasonable. Possessed of reason, persons can critically assess the alternatives from which they may choose; possessed of autonomy, they are free to select among them. Thus are persons morally responsible for what they do. It is because persons (and only persons) have the requisite capacities for moral agency, and because all nonpersons lack these capacities, that persons are said to enjoy the unique, superior moral status that they do. Moreover, it is because persons (and only persons) share this unique, superior moral status that the factual approach sanctions the conclusion that persons (and only persons) can and do have rights.

I need to say something about the idea that persons are morally superior, that they occupy a moral status superior to that of everyone and everything else. Different people can interpret this idea differently, but in my view, a crucial consideration concerns how moral right and wrong will vary depending on whether our actions are directed toward persons or nonpersons. If persons occupy a superior moral status, then there will be some things we will not be free to do to them that we will be free to do to nonpersons. Where does our freedom end in the one case and extend in the other? That, as I say, is where different people might offer different answers. The one I propose takes the freedom routinely to harm as fundamental. If persons occupy a superior moral status, then whereas it would be wrong routinely to kill, disfigure, or otherwise harm them merely so that others will benefit, it would not be wrong routinely to do these same things to nonpersons. Indeed, if it were no less wrong to do these things in the case of nonpersons than it is in the case of persons, I would find it difficult to understand how anyone could intelligibly believe that persons are morally superior to nonpersons.

By my lights, then, ascribing a superior moral status to persons has logical connections to the moral tie, at least in this sense: all and only persons are covered by the moral tie. In other words, it is morally wrong routinely to override the rights of persons merely on the ground that others will benefit but permissible to do so with nonpersons. Possibly there are additional considerations that undergird the alleged moral superiority of persons. I have no quarrel with those who want to paint a more complete conceptual picture. All I wish to maintain, and (for my purposes here) all I do maintain, is that when we attempt to explain the idea that persons have a superior moral status, the moral tie plays the role I have identified.

Like the moral approach, the factual approach has certain advantages. For example, like the moral, the factual approach arguably provides a basis for saying (and explicating) why strapping teenagers and their middle-aged parents have rights, regardless of race, ethnicity, class, or sexual orientation. Moreover, the factual approach seems to have this advantage over the moral: it appears to answer the question, "Which individuals have rights?" without having to ground its answer in the moral. Individuals have rights if and only if they are persons, and individuals are persons if and only if they are rational and autonomous, something that (borderline cases to one side) arguably can be determined using ordinary empirical measures of rationality and autonomy. Whether any given individual *has* these characteristics (let us assume) is something we can know without having to make any moral judgment, including in particular the judgment contained in the moral tie.

On reflection, however, the moral neutrality of the factual approach proves to be as much a liability as an asset. Suppose some individual A has the preferred set of characteristics (rationality and autonomy) said to define personhood. Then (let us assume) it is true as a matter of fact that A is a person. That agreed, a daunting problem presents itself. Precisely because the characteristics that define personhood are themselves nonmoral, to classify A as a person does not tell us anything about A's status as a *rights-bearer*. To move from the proposition "A is a person" (that is, "A is rational and autonomous") to "A has rights," the suppressed premise, "All those individuals who are rational and autonomous (all those who are persons) have rights," needs to be justified. Not only is this a tall order, as the riddled remains of past attempts by our philosophical predecessors amply demonstrate; it is an order that cannot be filled if we avoid having any dealings with "the moral." Unless I am mistaken, attributions of moral rights cannot possibly be justified if they are not grounded in moral considerations.

Similar remarks apply when we consider the belief in the unique, superior moral status persons are supposed to enjoy. From the proposition "A is rational and autonomous" nothing whatever follows concerning A's moral status, least of all that this status is both unique and superior. Moreover, while it is true (given certain conceptions of moral agency) that all and only persons are moral agents, it does not follow that all and only persons are morally superior to everyone and everything else. Clearly, the move from "A is a person" to "A enjoys a morally superior status" will require a good deal by way of foundational moral theorizing. The factual approach, as sketched here, does not so much avoid the moral as delay the need to deal with it.

It is important that I not be misunderstood here. I am not saying that facts have no bearing on the moral judgments we make. For example, in his widely praised book *Created from Animals: The Moral Implications of Darwinism* (1990), James Rachels convincingly shows how facts can undermine cherished moral convictions. Statements of fact do not entail statements of value, he concedes, so the seventeenth-century Scottish philosopher David Hume is correct when he insists that we cannot derive an "ought" from an "is." It does not follow, however, that facts are irrelevant to values. If my reasons for believing X are a, b, and c, and if you are able to demonstrate that a, b, and c are false or lack credible support, then you have undermined my belief in X; this is no less true if what I believe is a matter of value and my reasons for believing it are matters of fact.

Rachels's interest in the way facts can undermine values is at the heart of his study of Darwinism's relevance to morality in general and its relevance to powerful religious conceptions of the origin and value of human life in particular. Many people, probably the majority of Americans, believe that human life is uniquely valuable because humans are the result of a special creation by God. Darwin's teachings challenge this belief. Human life is not the result of a special creation by God. On the contrary, human life evolved over time, and we, the apes, and the monkeys are the descendants of a common ancestor.

Suppose the basic thrust of Darwin's theory is correct. If it is—and, like Rachels, I come down strongly on Darwin's side on this matter—then Darwinism effectively undermines the belief that human life is uniquely valuable *if* this belief rests on the claim that human life originated because of a special creation of God. The truth of Darwinism does not prove conclusively that human life is not uniquely valuable; that is, the statements "Humans are descended from the same ancestors as monkeys and apes" and "Human life evolved over time" do not entail the statement "Human life is not uniquely valuable." As a matter of logic, it remains possible that human life is uniquely valuable even if it did not originate as a special creation by God; what is not possible is that human life is uniquely valuable because humans are the result of God's special creation.

In addition to undermining moral convictions, facts are relevant to values in other ways, including questions about who possesses rights. For example, if we were to agree that (a) all and only persons possess rights, and (b) all and only persons are rational and autonomous, then establishing who is rational and autonomous would be decisively relevant to determining who possesses rights.

I take it to be well established, then, that facts are relevant to values. Nevertheless, I take it to be no less evident that the relevance of facts to values does not adequately address the problems I believe are endemic to the factual approach. This approach assumes that we can determine who possesses rights without making any moral judgments; all we need do is determine who possesses a given set of characteristics (for example, reason and autonomy); once we have done that, we will know who enjoys the status of a rights-holder.

This cannot be correct. To identify someone as a bearer of rights is to say something different from and more than what is said by offering a factual description. To possess rights is to occupy a singular moral status, one feature of which is captured by the earlier discussion of rights as a trump. If Smith and Jones have rights, then it is wrong routinely to treat them in a variety of disrespectful ways merely so that others will benefit. No manner of factual descriptions on their own can confer this status on anyone. To make this clearer, suppose Smith is rational and autonomous (a person), whereas Jones, because he is neither, is a nonperson. That much granted, it remains to be determined whether either or both of them have rights, and merely to be told that Smith has some empirically verifiable characteristics that Jones lacks will leave the matter undetermined. Granted, *if* we have already decided to base the possession of rights on the possession of rationality and autonomy, *then* we will have grounds for affirming rights in Smith's case while denying them in Jones's, but determining *whether* to base the possession of rights on one set of factual characteristics rather than another is not itself something that can be settled merely by adducing more and more facts. That is something that requires our making one or more moral judgments, judgments that declare what characteristics are to count as grounding the possessing of rights in particular. Just as the description of a good golf swing is not itself a good (or bad) golf swing, so our judgment concerning the basis for possessing rights, while it may cite the possession of some factual characteristics as decisive, is not itself a factual judgment. To single out some individuals as deserving of respectful treatment that is not owed to others is to confer on them a privileged moral status, something that requires making a moral judgment and something for which adducing relevant facts can never substitute.

Assessment of the Two Approaches

As has been discussed, both approaches, the moral no less than the factual, have crowded agendas that call for a serious (and no doubt protracted) consideration of a host of vexing problems. Against this backdrop of unfinished business, is there anything that can be said in favor of one or the other approach? I think there is.

The two approaches are demonstrably inconsistent, and in a fashion that favors the moral over the factual approach. This is perhaps clearest when we consider the moral status of young children. Given the moral approach, these children have a right to life or a right to bodily integrity, for example, only if it is wrong routinely to kill them or to disfigure their bodies merely on the ground that others will benefit. Myself, I profoundly hope and (in my more optimistic moments) assume that all people of goodwill agree that routinely harming young children for this reason is wrong. I grant that in *some* circumstances infanticide, for example, may be permissible. What I do not grant, and what I hope and assume every person of goodwill joins me in denying, is that there is nothing wrong in *routinely* harming young children merely on the ground that others will benefit.

Of course, even if it were true that all humanity speaks with one voice on this matter, that would not prove that humanity's voice speaks truly. Those, like myself, who believe that moral judgments can be true or false face a deep and broad challenge, one that for obvious reasons I cannot attempt to meet on this occasion. Instead, what I ask here is that we assume for the sake of argument that it is wrong routinely to kill or in other ways harm young children merely so that others will benefit. That much granted, the moral approach provides a basis for saying (and explicating) why young children possess rights. They possess rights because, as is true of all rights-holders, it is wrong routinely to harm them merely so that others will benefit.

The factual approach, even if we grant (what, as already noted, is disputable) that all and only persons have rights, does not permit this conclusion. If A is a person if and only if A is rational and autonomous, then young children do not have rights. Indeed, lacking as they are in these capacities, they cannot have rights.

Thus the inconsistency: given the moral approach, young children can and do have rights; given the factual approach, young children do not and cannot have rights. On the basis of this difference alone, is there any reason to prefer the one approach over the other? I think there is.

Of the two ways of approaching the question before us, it is difficult to muster much enthusiasm for the factual. If anything is false or unfounded morally, it surely must be that it is not morally wrong (that it is morally permissible) routinely to kill or otherwise harm young children merely so that others will benefit. Any view regarding human rights that entails that such behavior *is* permissible has (to understate the case) little to recommend it. Of course, to make this judgment does not prove that the moral approach is to be preferred over every other possible approach; what it does show is that we have *a* reason to prefer it over the factual.

Proponents of the factual approach could argue that we have less. Anyone who favors this approach can have recourse to one or another of several putative explanations concerning why this approach is not committed to permitting routine harm done to young children merely so that others will benefit. Some of these possible explanations are grounded in claims made about these children themselves; others are grounded in claims made about human persons. I begin with the former.

Defending the Factual Approach: Focusing on Children

Young children are neither rational nor autonomous. That is a fact. But (it may be alleged) it is also a fact that they *will* acquire these capacities (and thus will become persons) in the course of their normal development. That being so, someone who accepts the factual approach might maintain that we should treat young children, because they are *potential* persons, as if they are actual persons and thus as if they actually have rights. This much allowed, proponents of the factual approach could maintain that it is wrong routinely to harm young children merely so that others will benefit.

Although appealing, this response has implications that many will find unacceptable. If young children should be treated as if they have rights (because they have the potential to acquire those characteristics said to be definitive of personhood), then it will be difficult to avoid prohibiting the vast majority of elective abortions (because the vast majority of human fetuses also have the potential to acquire these characteristics). Possibly most or even all elective abortions are morally wrong because they violate the fetus's right to life. Then again, possibly they are not. What is certain is that (1) advocates of the view that all and only persons have rights characteristically wish to disassociate themselves from the view that routinely permitting elective abortion is wrong (Warren 1973) and that (2) these same advocates will have a difficult time explaining why young children who have the potential to become persons should be treated as if they have rights, whereas human fetuses, who also have this potential, may be treated as if they do not.

A second, no less serious challenge begins by noting that, tragically, some human children lack the potential to become persons in the course of their normal development. These children need not lack every characteristic that various accounts postulate as essential to personhood. For example, they are not only in the world but aware of it: they see and hear and feel, for example. Moreover, they enjoy some things, while others cause them pain; some things they experience frighten them, while others provide comfort and assurance. Not able to use a language such as English or German, these children nevertheless can communicate their desires and preferences, their joys and sorrows, their recognition of those familiar to them and their suspicion of strangers. Though they are limited when it comes to higher-order cognitive abilities, it makes perfectly good sense to view these children as having both a unified psychological presence in the world and an experiential welfare. They are each the subject of a life that fares well or ill for them, logically independently of considerations about how valuable they might be to others. Nevertheless, what these children do not have, and what they never will have, is the potential to become rational, autonomous agents. Lacking as they are in these crucial respects, these children never will become—and never can become—persons.

What, then, should be said in response to the idea of routinely killing or in other ways harming these children merely so that others will benefit? If these children are not persons, if because of their deficiencies they never will and never can become persons, and if all and only persons can and do have rights, then these children are not now and never will become rights-bearers. As such, given the factual approach, nothing about the moral status of these children themselves precludes the permissibility of routinely killing or otherwise harming them merely so that others will benefit. To the extent that we wish to distance ourselves from (what I assume people of goodwill view as) this presumably morally otiose proposal, we are right to insist that the factual approach must do better than this.

Defending the Factual Approach: Focusing on Persons

Perhaps a better way to defend the factual approach can be found by grounding protection for young children not in claims made about these children themselves but in claims made about *other* human beings—namely, those humans who, like us, are paradigmatic persons. After all, this line of thought begins (Narveson 1977), adults have an interest in having children treated well. Parents and grandparents arguably see this most clearly, but even most people who do not have children recognize that society in general is better off if children are protected against routine assaults on their lives and bodies. In general, abused children become abusers as adults, which is reason enough not to harm them routinely merely so that others will benefit.

I find this way of responding to the challenge at hand strongly counterintuitive. The reason we ought not to kill or otherwise harm young children, it seems to me, must lie in concern for the children themselves, not in the effects such acts will have on others, including society in general. That the factual approach would be obliged to change the moral focus, taking attention away from the children and directing it to the interests of others, is a symptom that something has gone badly wrong.

The following example suggests just how wrong. Tragically, as we know all too well, the Nazis treated young Jewish children in unspeakably horrible ways. Along with millions of adults, children were killed and otherwise harmed for the worst of reasons—namely, unrestrained racial and ethnic hatred. Sometimes, however, as in the case of the infamous experiments carried out by physicians and researchers, there was a semblance of ostensible justification: the experiments were conducted to find cures and devise treatments that would benefit Nazis and their progeny. Now if the basis for deciding how children may be treated is to be found not in considerations of concern for these children themselves but instead in considerations that focus on how others will be affected, and if it had turned out that the Nazis benefited from routinely killing or in other ways harming Jewish children in medical experiments, then what are we to say? That it was perfectly all right for the Nazis to carry out their heinous research protocols using Jewish children? If advocates of the factual approach change the focus from the children to benefits for others, I do not see how they can have a basis for denouncing an affirmative answer to this question as in principle unacceptable.

Compare this finding with the implications of the moral approach. Was it wrong routinely to kill or otherwise harm Jewish children in medical research that sought to benefit Nazis and their progeny? I hope and trust others will join me in saying, "Yes, beyond any doubt." Did these children, then, have rights? Given the moral approach, the answer is, "Yes, most assuredly." Which, then, is better, an approach to rights that fails to explain why it is wrong routinely to harm children of whatever race or ethnicity merely so that others will benefit, or an approach to rights that explains this? Surely the latter is preferable. Thus, even granting that the moral approach faces many difficult challenges, we have reason enough to prefer it over the factual approach.

The Rights of Nonhuman Animals

As already discussed, the moral approach recognizes the rights of individuals who are not persons, including children who can never become persons. I now want to show how the consistent use of this same approach leads us to recognize the rights of a large number of other-than-human animals.

People of goodwill can and often do disagree about what is right and wrong. Perhaps nothing illustrates this better than the protracted debate over the morality of abortion. Some people believe that, because human life begins at conception and all human life is sacred, abortion is murder. Others, citing the vast differences between a small group of undifferentiated cells and a fully formed human being (the pregnant woman), deny this. Those who accept the former view judge that it is wrong routinely to kill or in other ways harm human fetuses merely so that others will benefit; among those who accept the latter position, we find a different judgment. Viewed against the backdrop of this fundamental difference concerning what is morally permissible, it is perfectly intelligible and indeed predictable that one side to the abortion debate will attribute, and another deny, rights to human fetuses.

While people of goodwill can disagree about the morality of abortion, virtually all will agree that once born, children should not routinely be killed or otherwise harmed merely to benefit others. True, people of goodwill can disagree about the *reason* children should not be treated in this way, but all will agree that they should not. Moreover, the children who should be protected against such treatment include both those who have the potential to become persons and those who, while they possess some of the characteristics definitive of personhood, lack the potential to acquire the sort of rationality and autonomy that makes moral agency possible. Recall how these children were described: they are not only in the world but aware of it. Some things they experience are enjoyable; others cause them pain. Some things frighten them; others provide comfort and assurance. Not able to use a language such as English or German, they nevertheless can communicate their desires and preferences, their joys and sorrows, their recognition of those familiar to them and their suspicion of strangers. Though they are limited, certainly, it makes perfectly good sense to view these children as having both a unified psychological presence in the world and an experiential welfare. They are each the subject of a life that fares well or ill for them, logically independently of how valuable they are to others. Nevertheless, what these children do not have, and what they never will have, is the potential to become rational, autonomous agents. Lacking as they are in these crucial respects, these children can never become persons. Notwithstanding this grim picture, I assume that all people of goodwill agree that these children should not be routinely killed or otherwise harmed merely to benefit others. In this sense, the moral consensus concerning these children is strikingly different from the moral discord concerning human fetuses.

Fallible creatures that we are, not all our moral judgments will be true, even assuming that some are. As noted earlier, uncertainty about which moral judgments are true is a serious challenge for both the moral and the factual approaches. Without attempting to address the full measure of this challenge here, this much is certain: the moral beliefs we accept cannot all be true if they include two or more inconsistent beliefs. This much, too, seems clear: our commitment to search for and, when we find them, to address such inconsistencies offers a fair indication of the seriousness with which we respond to the challenge to develop an informed, thoughtful moral outlook.

A common inconsistency concerns beliefs about the moral status of human children, on the one hand, and beliefs about the moral status of nonhuman animals, on the other. How should we judge the moral status of nonhuman animals who resemble human children in the relevant respects, that is, those animals who are in the world and aware of it; who experience some things as enjoyable and others as painful; who can be frightened and comforted; who are able to communicate their desires and preferences, their joys and sorrows, and their recognition of those familiar to them and their suspicion of strangers; and who, like human children, have both a unified psychological presence in the world and an experiential welfare over time—in short, those animals who are each the subject of a life that fares well or ill for them, logically independently of how valuable they are to others? If it is wrong routinely to kill or in other ways harm human children having these characteristics merely so that others will benefit, and if this is a sufficient basis for their possessing rights; then how can we avoid reaching the same conclusions with regard to those nonhuman animals who are like these children in the relevant respects? If these children have rights, how can we consistently refuse to recognize the rights of these animals?

One obvious way to attempt to avoid this conclusion is to deny that there are any nonhuman animals who have the previously mentioned characteristics. A handful of philosophers and scientists do persist in denying most if not all of these characteristics to other-than-human animals. Their numbers are already negligible and continue to dwindle as we learn more about other animals, including their evolutionary kinship with us. Both the best empirical data and our best explanatory theories support the judgment that vast numbers of nonhuman animals (mammals, birds, and other vertebrates, for starters) share the psychological characteristics in question (DeGrazia 1997).

A second way to try to avoid ascribing rights to nonhuman animals is to insist that rights belong exclusively to all humans. When we ask why this is so, however, the answers seem to be a muddle at best and prejudice masquerading as principle at worst. We are told, for example, that animals cannot have rights because rights "arise" in a human community (Cohen 1986). Do dogs, dolphins, dingoes, and dromedaries have the concept of a right? No. Do humans? Yes. Well then, we humans have rights whereas other animals do not.

Can things be that simple? I think not. By proving too much, this line of argument actually proves too little (if we count nothing as too little). Using this argument's logic, we can "prove" that dogs, dolphins, dingoes, and dromedaries do not have eyes, hearts, nerves, and genes, whereas we humans do, because we have the relevant concepts and they do not. There is, alas, hardly any limit to the absurdities a faulty form of argument can prove.

A third and, for my purposes, final way to attempt to avoid ascribing rights to nonhuman animals is to deny them in the case of human children. This response would have the desired effect of making our moral beliefs about children and animals consistent, but it would achieve this result at a very great price, since, as I have argued previously, we would no longer be able to say that it is wrong routinely to kill or otherwise harm children merely so that others will benefit. Speaking for myself, I do not believe we are morally free to exploit children in the ways this conclusion would sanction. And although I must stop well short of attempting to justify this judgment, I sincerely hope that others will agree. Moreover, if this much is granted, then the consistency we seek among our moral beliefs is to be found not by changing what we think about the way children may be treated but by changing our beliefs about the permissible treatment of other animals. Specifically, consistency is achieved by acknowledging that, just as it is wrong routinely to kill or otherwise harm children merely so that others will benefit, so it is wrong routinely to do this to relevantly similar animals, and for the same reason. Or (to express the same substantive point differently), consistency is achieved by recognizing that both young children and relevantly similar nonhuman animals have rights.

Limits and Implications

Throughout this chapter I have stressed the amount of work remaining to be done if the conclusions I favor are to receive a more thorough justification. I have considered only two of an indefinite number of possible approaches to answering the question, "Who has rights?"; even in these two cases, I have left unanswered a number of important questions relating to the status and possible confirmation of moral judgments in particular. While openly admitting (indeed, insisting on) these limitations, I should emphasize in conclusion the possible significance of what I have shown.

Recall the third of the widely shared beliefs stated at the outset:

3. All persons, and only persons, do have rights.

If by *persons* we mean "rational and autonomous agents," if individuals have rights when it is wrong routinely to harm them merely so that others will benefit, and if it is wrong routinely to harm children (including those who lack the potential to become persons) for this reason, then it is false that all and only persons actually possess rights. Furthermore, if this proposition is false, then so is the second widely shared belief examined along the way—namely:

2. All persons, and only persons, can have rights.

Clearly, if nonpersons (for example, human infants) do have rights, then it is demonstrably false that only persons can have them.

What, then, of the first widely shared belief?

1. Compared with everyone and everything else, persons have a unique, superior moral status.

I have already offered considerations that seem to support attributing a unique moral status to persons. Arguably, it is true that all and only persons are moral agents—that all and only persons are morally responsible for what they do. However, our being unique in this respect does not entail that we therefore occupy a superior moral status. On the contrary, we have no claim to a moral status superior to that of those children whose moral status has been under review. Just as it is wrong routinely to harm human persons merely so that others will benefit, so it is wrong routinely to harm human children for this same reason. Moreover, just as it is true (assuming that it is) that human persons have rights, so it is true that these children do, too. The unique capacities for moral agency that persons possess do not confer a uniquely superior moral status on all and only persons. From the moral point of view, it is time we put people in their place.

Assuming that the preceding argument is sound, however, it is also time we did the same for those other-than-human animals who share with persons the equal moral status that is conferred by possessing equal moral rights, a finding that cannot help but add to the many challenges facing those scientists who use these animals in their research. Many are the reasons these animals are used. Tradition is one; the search for knowledge for knowledge's sake is another, as are the possible benefits others may derive from discoveries to be made. Indeed, of all the possible bases of justification, the appeal to the benefits derived is both the most common and the most compelling. Let the appeals to tradition, the intrinsic value of knowledge, and other putative justifications of animal-model research (for example, those of an economic nature) be set to one side; I hazard the judgment that most of those who favor such research suppose the benefits claimed in its behalf to be enough. This is why, in their view, it is not wrong to kill or otherwise harm nonhuman animals merely so that others will benefit.

And there's the rub. If we cannot justify routinely harming rights-bearers merely because others will benefit, if animals used in research are routinely harmed, and if these animals have rights, then we cannot justify such research merely by appealing to the benefits others might or will derive. Once this source of possible justification is denied, however, it is difficult to imagine how else such research could possibly be justified. Appeals to tradition and the intrinsic value of knowledge, for example, fail to provide even a shred of justification for violating someone's rights. As for economic considerations, those who would walk down this path, thinking it provides a means of justifying routine violations of rights in the present, would do well to review the moral atrocities this sort of thinking has been thought to justify in the past.

It remains open to those who favor such research to ground their justification not in the benefits allegedly secured but in the word of some god who (let us suppose) has decreed that it is perfectly all right routinely to kill and in other ways to harm animals in laboratories merely so that others will benefit—a proposal that, if taken seriously, seems to me to provide not a justification for animal-model research but a good reason to believe in no god rather than in this one. But that is another, longer story, suitable for some other possible occasion.

Works Cited

Cohen, Carl. 1986. "The Case for the Use of Animals in Biomedical Research." *New England Journal of Medicine* 315, no. 14:865–70.

DeGrazia, David. 1997. "Great Apes, Dolphins, and the Concept of Personhood." *Southern Journal of Philosophy* 35, no. 3:301–20.

Dworkin, Ronald. 1977. *Taking Rights Seriously.* London: Duckworth.

Narveson, Jan. 1977. "Animal Rights." *Canadian Journal of Philosophy* 7, no. 1:161–78.

Rachels, James. 1990. *Created from Animals.* Oxford: Oxford University Press.

Regan, Tom. 1983. *The Case for Animal Rights.* Berkeley: University of California Press.

Warren, Mary Ann. 1973. "The Moral and Legal Status of Abortion." *Monist* 57, no. 1:43–61.

6

PATTERNS OF RESISTANCE

One of life's special satisfactions comes from receiving an honor without having the slightest inkling that it was in the offing. This certainly was true in my case when, in the fall of 1994, I received an invitation to deliver the Eighth Annual Dunbar Lecture at Millsaps College, in Jackson, Mississippi. Up to then, I had had no contact with this fine institution, and to say that I was surprised by the invitation is to understate the case.

As it happened, the obligation to deliver the Dunbar Lecture coincided with work I had planned but never commenced. For several years I had been teaching a course I call "The Moral Community: The Struggle for Freedom and Equality in America." Even before then, I had been reading widely in the areas covered in the course—in Native American and African American studies, for example. But whereas the syllabus was rounding into reasonably good shape, I had not written anything that synthesized what I had been studying. The surprise invitation from the good people at Millsaps proved to be the push I needed.

The course I teach is multidisciplinary in nature. For one thing, we read a lot of history. This by itself is unusual, possibly even unique, for a course in moral philosophy. If I have learned anything during my more than thirty-five years of college teaching, however, it is that many students have a poor background in history; if I have learned a second thing, it is that we can have at most a superficial understanding of the major moral issues we face today—such issues as abortion and affirmative action—if we know little about what happened yesterday. Granted, knowing how, when, and why abortion and affirmative action became the divisive matters they are does not answer the relevant moral questions associated with these practices, but not knowing the former all but guarantees that we will see only the forest and miss the moral trees.

Among the trees that will be missed is the enormous influence Christianity and science have had in shaping the American moral landscape. These two powerful institutions have sometimes been on the side of the right and the good, but as I attempt to document in these pages, history teaches that they have also frequently cast their lot with the worst, the most evil of human prejudices. To recognize that some of the best scientists and scores of the most learned Christians have offered robust defenses of evil may help make us more receptive to the possibility that the same thing could be happening today. The need to encourage young people to "question authority" was not a unique 1960s phenomenon.

In addition to presenting some of the many faces of evil against the backdrop of American history, these pages pose a personal question: how would we have responded to those prejudices that made slavery possible had we lived during slavery's reign in America? Would we have risen above the racism that created and sustained this "peculiar institution," or would we have sided with those who favored keeping millions of people in permanent bondage? The chapter concludes by describing one way we might find an answer.

This chapter is a modest revision of the text I prepared and in part read in my capacity as one of Millsaps College's Dunbar Lecturers. It has not been previously published.

Birth of a Nation

> *We hold these Truths to be self-evident, that all Men are created equal, that they are endowed by their Creator with certain unalienable Rights, that among these are Life, Liberty and the Pursuit of Happiness.*

These brave, defiant words are well known to virtually all Americans. A new nation was about to be born, founded on the principle of the inviolability of the individual, a nation whose government was called into being to protect "all men" in the possession of their rights rather than to dispense rights as those sitting in royal power saw fit. Seldom in history have the aspirations of freedom and equality been more eloquently expressed. No other words better capture what America was conceived to be at its inception and what it has struggled to become during the more than two hundred years of its history.

This history is both long and complicated. The battles fought, the elections waged, the inventions and technologies that changed not only where people work but what they do, the recurring waves of immigration and migration, the founding of cities and the recognition of states, the lands cleared and the roads built, the crops planted and the homes constructed, the biographies of the famous and the lives of ordinary people, the novels and poems written, the plays performed, the paintings exhibited—all this and much, much more would need to be included in an even modestly complete history of this country.

Blessedly, as a philosopher I am relieved that the challenge to tell this larger story is the proper habitat of historians. My interest on this occasion, though far more modest, is daunting enough. I want to consider only a few sentences, as it were, of the larger story of America, sentences that concern themes indigenous to the lines quoted previously. For while this nation was founded on the recognition of those "unalienable rights" enshrined in the Declaration of Independence, the plain fact is that not all humans, not even all men, were included under the rubric "all men."

"All Men"?

History removes any doubt about this. When the time came for the founding fathers to take the principles of the Declaration of Independence and forge them into this nation's Constitution and Bill of Rights, not all men or even all citizens were recognized as having the same rights. Native Americans certainly were not. African Americans certainly were not. Women of all races certainly were not. If not these people, however, then who were these "all men" whose rights were to be forever protected? The answer that the early history of the United States compels us to accept is all white men—more narrowly and precisely, all white male property owners.

For consider: both Washington and Jefferson, whom we honor with monuments in our nation's capitol, owned slaves, and although the framers of the Constitution ended the importation of slaves in 1808, those slaves already here (some 4 million by 1860) did not share in those inalienable rights enshrined in the Declaration of Independence. Moreover, Jefferson was so convinced of the inferiority of African Americans that he favored their involuntary recolonization: whether they wanted to or not, African Americans were to be sent back to Africa, whence they came. (Lincoln, honored with yet another national monument adorning the cityscape of Washington, D.C., was differently inclined. He thought the best solution to America's race problem was for free blacks to volunteer to leave the country; those free blacks who did not agree with him resisted because, in Lincoln's words, they acted from "an extremely selfish view" [Lincoln 1906:115].) As for women, it took an amendment to the Constitution in 1920, after more than seventy years of concerted effort, to secure for them the elementary right to vote.

So, no, the founding fathers did not mean everybody when they said "all men are created equal." And so it is that despite the stirring words of the Declaration of Independence, and notwithstanding the rousing sentiments expressed in the promise of "freedom and justice for all," this nation was founded on principles that, in the hands of the founding fathers, are noteworthy for their racism, sexism, and classism.

Accepting this (for many people) unsettling fact is essential if we are to understand not only what America was in the beginning but also what it has struggled to become historically. My remarks here explore some modest ways we might advance our understanding in this regard.

The Ideal Moral Community

One way to proceed is by utilizing the concept of the ideal moral community. Imagine a circle whose boundaries determine membership in the moral community. Those individuals who are members fall inside the circle and are viewed as equal to one another, enjoying the same moral status. Those individuals outside the circle are viewed as unequal to those inside and lack their moral status. In the *ideal* moral community, all those who should be recognized as members are so recognized. In other words, in the ideal moral community, no one is excluded from membership because of bias, prejudice, special interests, the sheer weight of custom, selfishness, or any other morally arbitrary reason.

If we recognize that, at its inception, the prevailing American conception of the moral community restricted membership to white men who owned property, then we can picture the American struggle for freedom and equality as the attempt to extend the boundaries of our imaginary circle— to enlarge its diameter so that human beings previously excluded from membership (e.g., for reasons of prejudice or ignorance) come to be included.

Defending the Status Quo

How do the beneficiaries of membership in a less than ideal moral community act to retain their privileged status? One obvious way is by using force, including the state's police powers. Again, history has a lesson to teach. Among those Americans who have agitated for a more inclusive moral community, some have been beaten, arrested, sent to prison, tortured, and executed; their homes have been destroyed, and their family members have been separated, harassed, injured, and even killed. The more oppressive and powerful the government, the more common the use of force is likely to be. There is no question that, during the past two hundred years, the U.S. government and the governments of the several states have used force to defend the interests of those occupying a privileged moral status denied to others.

As important as the use of the state's coercive powers is, this is only a small part of the story. In general, these powers carry out policies that are adopted independently of these powers themselves. Whereas force can be and often is used to maintain the status quo, we must look beyond the use of force itself to explain why it is used for this purpose.

Part of that explanation will be found by attending to the contributions of two powerful institutions in American history. Christianity is one; science is the other. By limiting my remarks to these two institutions, I do not mean to suggest that no others contribute to preserving the moral status quo. Economic and political forces certainly do, as does the sheer power of custom, including popular culture—the media, the songs that are sung, the art of the times, even the cookie jars and banks people have in their homes. (Think of the popularity of images of Aunt Jemimah and black "lawn jockeys.") By focusing primarily on Christianity and science, I choose only two among many possible institutions that have contributed to the defense of excluding some from America's historical conception of the moral community—the community of moral equals.

I restrict my remarks here mainly to the dynamics of exclusion as this has affected the members of three groups: African Americans, women, and gays and lesbians. By omitting other groups (for example, the mentally ill and the physically disadvantaged) I do not mean to suggest that Christianity and science have not operated as forces of resistance to their inclusion in the moral community; limits of time, not of possibilities, oblige me to be selective in what I discuss. Nevertheless, near the end of my remarks I want to draw attention to the way these same institutions have functioned, and continue to function, as forces of resistance to a fourth, contemporary challenge to enlarge the boundaries of the moral community.

One other thing I will not be able to do—and this is something a fuller, more balanced story would have to include—is to highlight the positive role

Christianity and the scientific enterprise have played in moving America toward an expanded conception of the moral community. Our history is replete with people of the Christian faith and practitioners of science who have agitated against the bigotry of exclusion. This has been true of America in the past, and it remains true of America in the present. My very modest object here is to remind people of, to use Paul Harvey's famous words, "the rest of the story."

A Christian Slavery

It comes as a surprise to many people to learn that American slavery did not lack for Christian apologists, but Christian apologists there were, from both the North and the South and among both whites and blacks. The reverend George D. Armstrong's *Christian Doctrine of Slavery* is representative of those white southern Christians (Armstrong was the pastor of the First Presbyterian Church of Norfolk, Virginia, when his book was published in 1857) who defended the compatibility of slavery and Christian belief, while Jupiter Hammon, a life-long slave, is representative of those Christians of African ancestry who called on slaves to carry out their Christian duty to serve their masters.

Both Armstrong and Hammon rest their case on the Bible, not only what it says, but also what it does not. Among the relevant passages is this one from Paul's epistle to the Ephesians: "Slaves, obey your earthly masters with fear and trembling in singleness of heart, as you obey Christ; not only while being watched, and in order to please them, but as slaves of Christ, doing the will of God from the heart. Render service with enthusiasm, as to the Lord and not to men and women, knowing that whatever good we do, we shall receive the same from the Lord, whether we are slaves or free" (Eph. 6:5–8).

In view of this and similar passages of sacred scripture, Armstrong argues that the biblical message is unmistakable: there is nothing essential to the master-slave relationship that makes it sinful. If there were, Jesus would have condemned it, which he does not, and Paul would not have spoken of the slave's duty of obedience, which he does. True, slavery can involve sinful behavior, as when a master beats a slave for the pleasure of doing so, but according to Armstrong, the fact that masters can act sadistically, and thus sinfully, is not an essential but only an "incidental" aspect of slavery, something that in principle can be minimized as the institution approaches the ideal of (to use Armstrong's words) a "Christian slavery."

What would such a slavery be like? Armstrong's answer is premised on his belief that "the African slave, in our Southern States, [is] deeply degraded; the debasing effects of generations of sin . . . seem to have almost obliterated his humanity" (Armstrong 1969:137). Yet, he adds, the slave "is an immortal creature, one for whom God the Son died," and it is the responsibility of white Christians "to make him a worthy worshipper among God's people on earth, and a welcome worshipper among the ransomed in heaven" (134).

A "Christian slavery," then, would be one that brings slaves closer to Jesus while minimizing those evils "incidental" to the institution of slavery itself. According to Armstrong, in such a slavery "the master shall be required, by the laws of man as well as that of God, 'to give unto the slave that which is just and equal,' and the slave to render to the master a cheerful obedience and hearty service" (1969:134).

This is as far as the Christian church should go, in Armstrong's view. For the church to attempt to do more—in particular, for it to call for the abolition of slavery—"requires the Church to obtrude herself into the province of the State," an action that, according to Armstrong, would be "in direct violation of the ordinance of God." "The Church and State," Armstrong declares, "has each its own appropriate sphere of operation assigned it by God, and neither can innocently intrude itself into the province of the other" (1969:145).

Hammon is less concerned about the duties of the Christian church than he is about the duties of Christian slaves, which he discusses in *An Address to the Negroes of the State of New York*, published in 1787. Like Armstrong, Hammon has a dim view of his African brothers and sisters in bondage, regretting their "ignorance and stupidity, and the great wickedness of the most of [them]" (Hammon 1992:120). Commenting on the previously quoted passage from the apostle Paul, Hammon writes: "Here is a plain command of God for us to obey our masters. It may seem hard for us, if we think our masters wrong in holding us as slaves, to obey in all things, but who of us dare dispute God! He has commanded us to obey" (122).

Obey they must, Hammon believes, even if their masters treat them cruelly: "If a servant strives to serve his master . . . , I believe there are but few masters who would use such a servant cruelly. . . . If your master is really hard, unreasonable and cruel, there is no way so likely for you to convince him of it, as always to obey his commands, and try to serve him, and take care of his interest, and try to promote it all in your power" (1992:122). As

Hammon optimistically observes, "Good servants frequently make good masters" (ibid.).

In any event, to suffer cruelty in this world is of small consequence in Hammon's view. "We live so little time in this world," he writes, "that it is no matter how wretched and miserable we are, if it prepares us for heaven. What is forty, fifty, or sixty years, when compared to eternity . . . ? If God designs to set us free, he will do it, in his own time, and way" (1992:126). In the meantime, while God's decisions are awaited, Hammon counsels his fellow slaves as follows: "My brethren, it seems to me that there are no people that ought to attend to the hope of happiness in another world, so much as we. Most of us are cut off from comfort and happiness here in this world, and can expect nothing from it. Now seeing this is the case, why should we not take care to be happy after death. Why should we spend our whole lives in sinning against God: And be miserable in this world, and in the world to come" (ibid.).

In the case of both Rev. Armstrong and Jupiter Hammon, then, what we find are two concerned, sincere Christians who, for different reasons, accepted the American institution of slavery as being sanctified by God. In this structure, some are called to rule; others, to obey. Concerning those who rule, the Christian ethic requires generous beneficence; among those who are ruled, a cheerful obedience. Slaves are not to reason why they are in the situation they are, but neither are their masters to treat their human chattel thoughtlessly. On the contrary, the burden of the white owners—to bring their degraded, ignorant, stupid, wicked slaves to the acceptance of Jesus Christ as their redeemer—was in their minds a heavy one.

The Scientific Defense of Slavery

Whereas many Christians used the Bible to explain slavery's compatibility with their religious beliefs, it was more difficult to offer biblical proof that blacks are intellectually inferior to whites. Enter science, particularly comparative anatomy and physiology. What the Bible could not prove, some dedicated, devout scientists could. None was more dedicated or devout than the physician J. H. Van Evrie.

Among Van Evrie's widely read and influential scientific treatises is a work entitled *White Supremacy and Negro Subordination; or, Negroes a Subordinate Race and (so-called) Slavery its Normal Condition*, first published before the Civil War. After the manner of the reputable scientist, Van Evrie reduces truth to what is quantitatively measurable. What he chose to measure was the size (the physical mass) of the brain compared to the size of the body.

Van Evrie found that whites and blacks have about the same body size but differ in brain size. When Van Evrie finished his calculations, he found that the brain size of blacks was on average 10–15 percent smaller than that of whites. In Van Evrie's view, the existence of smaller brains scientifically explains why blacks as a race are mentally inferior to whites. Given Van Evrie's calculations, an adult black male approximates the intelligence of a seven-month-old white fetus.

Van Evrie also uses his small-brain theory to explain why blacks cannot grasp "abstract ideas," which in turn explains why they cannot read, write, or speak properly. When the linguistic skills of individual blacks are offered as counterinstances to his findings, Van Evrie replies that, like trained parrots, who do not understand what they say but who say it admirably well nonetheless, blacks who are able to use a language exhibit "borrowed," not "real," knowledge.

Why are things the way they are? Why are the members of one race mentally superior to those of other races (for, as I will show momentarily, Van Evrie does not restrict his theory of human intelligence to whites and blacks only)? Van Evrie believes that science cannot answer this question. Only religion can. And religion's answer is simple: whites have larger brains and are mentally superior to other races because God made things this way. All an appropriately humble, dedicated, devout scientist like Van Evrie can do is confirm that God's plans have been realized.

There is, then, a distinctively Van Evrian response to the suggestion that African Americans be recognized as the moral equals of whites. Not only would attempts to achieve such equality be "folly"; they would also be "impious," since, in trying to make equal what God has made unequal, we would be acting against the divine will (Van Evrie 1868:130).

The same is only slightly less true in the case of Native Americans. According to Van Evrie, whereas their brain size is on average less than whites', it is larger than blacks'. Nevertheless, the size of their brains shows that Indians, too, are incapable of understanding the world and knowing how to find their way around in it. When the ruins of advanced civilizations in Central and South America were adduced as proof that Indians founded, constructed, and sustained civilized ways of life long before white settlement, Van Evrie replied that his theories demonstrate just the opposite. Because their brain size proves that Indians are incapable of migration, Van Evrie confidently asserts that, when God created them, he must have placed them where white people found them—namely, in North, Central, and South America. As for the architectural ruins of advanced civilizations, Van Evrie no less confidently maintains that the existence of these ruins proves that white people must have arrived in Central and South American much earlier than many people thought, only to have migrated elsewhere at some time in the distant past. Whatever the alleged facts to the contrary, Van Evrie's theory proves their falsehood.

Today, looking back from a vantage point that enables us to know a good deal about the migratory routes to North, Central, and South America, we may find it difficult to take Van Evrie's ideas seriously. Many informed scientists of his day did, however, as did many other people, both those who preached the Christian Gospel and those who heard it.

Van Evrie was hardly alone in rendering a dispassionate, objective, scientific confirmation of the natural inferiority of African Americans. His contemporary Samuel Cartwright, a well-regarded physician from Louisiana, weighed in with his explanation of what he called "the peculiarities of the Negro race." Two ailments, *drapetomania* and *dysthesia ethiopica*, were especially troublesome. Drapetomania was manifested by a single symptom: slaves suffering from this malady wanted to run away. By contrast, signs of dysthesia ethiopica (also known as "rascality") were numerous and included talking back, fighting with masters, refusing to work, destroying property, and insensibility to pain. "When the unfortunate individual is subjected to punishment," Cartwright writes, "he neither feels pain of any consequence . . . [nor experiences] any resentment more than stupid sulkiness. In some cases . . . there appears to be an almost total loss of feeling" (in Gould 1981:71). "Like children," he writes, slaves are "constrained by unalterable physiological laws, to love those in authority over them. Hence, from a law of nature, the Negro can no more help loving a kind master, than a child can help loving her that gives it suck" (ibid.)

After emancipation medical opinion continued to be enlisted in support of judging blacks inferior to whites—and, as a corollary, as a principled, scientific basis for keeping the races segregated. People of real prominence in the field of medicine (G. Stanley Hall and William McDougal, for example) maintained that whites had advanced further than blacks on the evolutionary scale; that blacks are by nature prone to schizophrenia; and that blacks, because of their "happy-go-lucky" natures, are immune to depression. Because of blacks' natural inferiority, antimiscegenation laws could be and were defended as necessary public health measures.

One might think that medical defenses of racial prejudice are a thing of the distant past. Not so. By way of example, consider these observations by the American psychologist Hope Landrine:

> Contemporary clinicians, using a different language, appear to have maintained these racist concepts. They have argued that Blacks are lacking in ego strength and are culturally deprived, nonverbal, concrete, hostile, unmotivated, religious, and paranoid while at the same time essentially immune to depression. This immunity is no longer attributed to their happy-go-lucky nature but to their having nothing to lose—no jobs, property, or esteem. . . . When Wilson and Lantz theorized that a successful civil rights movement would create madness in Blacks because of the loss of a "well defined status," they echoed the notion that freedom seeking and protest are synonymous with psycho pathology for Blacks. The etiology was no longer *dysthesia ethiopica*. A 1967 article on the role of brain disease in urban riots, published in the Journal of the American Medical Association, pointed to a modern neurological disorder, *temporal lobe dysfunction*, for which recommended treatment, for Blacks, was psycho surgery. (Landrine 1988:39–40)

For my purposes, recognizing the biases behind Van Evrie's scientific theory and the prejudices that flavored both Armstrong's and Hammon's biblical defenses of slavery is less important than recognizing both science and religion as powerful forces that some individuals have used to defend the exclusion of African Americans from membership in the community of equals—the moral community.

Keeping Women in Their (Proper) Place

A similar pattern of resistance appears in the case of the women's' movement. For many of us alive today, it is difficult to imagine how things were for women in America as recently as a hundred and fifty years ago. At that time women lacked most of the rights we now take for granted. Not only were they legally barred from voting; in addition, they could not divorce their husbands or retain legal custody of a child if their husbands divorced them. On entering into marriage, they lost any right to property, including property bequeathed to them through inheritance. With few exceptions opportunities for higher education were denied to the members of the "fairer sex" (Oberlin College was the first to admit women, doing so in 1833, and by 1885 Smith, Wellesley, Vassar, Bryn Mawr, and Mills Colleges had opened their doors to women). As for the professions—law, medicine, science, and the ministry, for example—women were denied entry to them throughout most of the nineteenth century. A woman's place—her proper "sphere," to use the language of the time—was in the privacy of the home. The larger public "sphere" beyond the home was reserved for men.

Thomas R. Dew, in his "Dissertation on the Characteristic Differences between the Sexes," published in 1835, offers a representative statement of the ideology of the two spheres. "The relative position of the sexes in the social and political world," Dew writes,

> may certainly be looked upon as the result of organization. The greater physical strength of man, enables him to occupy the foreground in the picture. He leaves the domestic scenes; he plunges into the turmoil and bustle of an active, selfish world; in his journey through life, he has to encounter innumerable difficulties, hardships and labors which constantly beset him. His mind must be nerved against them. Hence courage and boldness are his attributes. It is his province, undismayed, to stand against the rude shocks of the world; to meet with a lion's heart, the dangers which threaten him. . . . [As for woman], her inferior strength and sedentary habits confine her within the domestic circle; she is kept aloof from the bustle and storm of active life; she is not familiarized to the out of door dangers and hardships of a cold and scuffling world: timidity and modesty are her attributes. (Dew 1835:493)

Pity the poor woman! What is she to do to guard herself against the cruelty of the world outside the home? Dew, a respected president of the College of William and Mary and the author of popular proslavery pamphlets, has an answer: "In the great strife which is constantly going forward around her, there are powers engaged which her inferior physical strength prevents her from countering. . . . men must be engaged in her cause" (1835:493).

Dew insists that the differences that separate the sexes are not meant to denigrate the female. "Grace, modesty and loveliness are the charms which constitute her power," he writes, adding that woman's power "is more emblematic of that of divinity: it subdues without effort." Granted, woman "may pursue her studies," but "not . . . with a view to triumphing in the senate chamber—not with a view to forensic display—not with a view of leading armies into combat" (1835:493). If not for these goals, however, then why should a woman pursue her studies? Only for the purpose of adding "delight and charm [to] all who breathe the atmosphere in which she moves" (494). In other words, women should attend to their studies just to the extent that, by the graceful, modest, and lovely display of their knowledge, they delight and charm men.

Not everyone accepted the two-spheres ideology. Notable women in the nineteenth century, including the Grimké sisters, Sarah and Angelina, dared to break the gender barrier and enter the realm of political debate. A *Boston Post* editorial of the time responded to women's roles in the antislavery movement in these terms: "Why are all the old hens abolitionists? Because not being able to obtain husbands they think they may stand a chance for a Negro, if they can make amalgamation [integration] possible?" (in Nie 1977:6).

Some women, as well as some men, already involved in the antislavery movement began to agitate on behalf of women's suffrage. Predictably, those who did were objects of derision in the popular press. By way of example, here are some excerpts from a *New York Herald* editorial, "The Woman's Rights Convention—The Last Act of the Drama," dated September 12, 1852.

> Who are these women? . . . Some of them are old maids, whose personal charms were never very attractive, and have been sadly slighted by the masculine gender in general; . . . some [of them] nature appears to have made a mistake in their gender—mannish women, like hens that crow. . . . So much for the women active in the suffragette movement.

As for the men, this same editorial continues:

> [They] shall be consigned to [their] proper sphere—nursing the babies, washing the dishes, mending stockings, and sweeping the house. . . . Of the male sex who attend these Conventions . . . , the majority are henpecked husbands, and all of them wear petticoats.

Obviously, the editorial writer regarded the very idea of equality for women as absurd.

> How did woman first become subject to man as she now is all over the world? By her nature, her sex, just as the Negro is and always will be, to the end of time, inferior to the white race, and therefore doomed to subjection; but happier than she would be in any other condition, just because it is the law of her nature.

These were hard times for the women and men who campaigned for a more inclusive, gender-blind conception of the moral community. Currents deeper than the printed words of editorials in the popular press resisted change. Like the social arrangements that excluded African Americans, the ideology that divided men and women into separate spheres had its roots in the way the Bible was read and assertions that scientists claimed to have proved.

Christian Defenses of the Two Spheres

Concerning the Bible, much was made of the belief that Eve was created from one of Adam's ribs in order that the original man might have a help-mate, an image that was repeatedly interpreted to mean "someone created to serve man." Orestes A. Brownson, writing in the *Catholic World* of May 1869, paints the prevailing biblical portrait of the sphere for which God created woman: "Woman was created to be a wife and a mother; that is her destiny. To that destiny all her instincts point, and for it nature has specially qualified her. Her proper sphere is home, and her proper function is the care of the household, to manage a family, to take care of children, and attend to their early training. . . . She was born to be a queen in her own household, and to make home cheerful, bright and happy" (1905:389).

To those who called for educational opportunities for women, Brownson replies: "We do not believe women, unless we acknowledge individual exceptions, are fit to have their own head. . . . revelation asserts, and universal experience proves that the man is the head of the woman, and that the woman is for the man, not the man for the woman; and [man's] greatest error [is] . . . that he be deprived of his reason, by woman. It was through the seductions of the woman, herself seduced by the serpent, that man fell, and brought sin and all our woe into the world" (1885:403).

According to Brownson, an informed reading of the Bible teaches that God gave woman those qualities that "fit her to be a help-mate of man, to be the mother of his children, to be their nurse, their early instructress, their guardian, their life-long friend; and to be [man's] companion, his comforter, his consoler in sorrow, his friend in trouble, his ministering angel in sickness" (1885:403). These are the roles of woman, as biblically sanctioned.

Were woman to stray beyond these divinely ordained roles—were she to pursue "an independent existence" where she would be "free to follow her own fancies and vague longings, her own ambition and natural love of power, without masculine direction or control"—she would exist "out of her element" and become "a social anomaly, sometimes a hideous monster, which men seldom are, excepting through a woman's influence" (Brownson 1885:403). What is more, to permit women to trespass into the public world divinely ordained for men only would be to allow first the weakening and then the destruction of "the Christian family." As Brownson warns, "when the family goes, the nation goes too, or ceases to be worth preserving" (Brownson 1905:388).

Scientific Defenses of the Two Spheres

Brownson and others who used biblical justifications for denying women rights that (some) men shared could appeal to revelation as the authority on which their judgment rested. Not so the men of science. As in Van Evrie's scientific validation of the divine order, they needed some measurable, quantifiable basis for restricting women to the private sphere of the home. Scientists from the eighteenth century onward saw themselves to be more than equal to the task.

The alarm sounded by the physician R. R. Coleman is representative.

> Women beware. You are on the brink of destruction: You have hitherto been engaged in crushing your waists; now you are attempting to culti-vate your mind: You have been merely dancing all night in the foul air of the ball-room; now you are beginning to spend your mornings in study. You have been incessantly stimulating your emotions with con-certs and operas, with French plays, and French novels; now you are exerting your understanding to learn Greek, and solve problems in Eu-clid. Beware! Science pronounces that the woman who studies is lost! (in Ehrenreich and English 1978:115)

Coleman's warning should be understood in context. Nineteenth-cen-tury (male) physicians and other scientists viewed the human body as the site of antagonism between the brain, representing a later stage of evolution, and the reproductive organs, representing an earlier stage. Well-meaning doc-tors advised men to regulate their sexual appetites so that the power of their brains, which they needed in the competitive, calculating world outside the home, could be utilized optimally. They strenuously discouraged an overly active sex life, including masturbation, where a man's reproductive "seed," like Onan's in the Old Testament, falls on "barren ground." Women, how-ever, were advised to commit themselves to their uteruses and to resist the temptations of the brain. A woman's offering energy to the brain function was seen as the female counterpart to a man's spilling his seed on barren ground.

Indeed, one Dr. Edward H. Clark, in his book *Sex in Education, or a Fair Chance for the Girls*, argues—presumably on the basis of precise measure-ments—that improper use of the brain by women causes their uteruses to atrophy (in Ehrenreich and English 1978:115). Moreover, G. Stanley Hall, the first president of the American Psychological Association, found that the more women learned, the more they risked losing their "mammary function" (in ibid.:116): women who were educated could not lactate and thus could not nurse their babies . . . if they had any. Hall and his colleagues were convinced that the scientific data demonstrated that educated women were slackards in just this regard. An influential 1895 study (see ibid.) proved that college-educated women were far less likely to marry than other women (28 percent versus 80 percent, respectively) and that those college-educated women who did marry were bearing fewer children. Understandably, therefore, the scientific opinion prevalent throughout the nineteenth and well into the twentieth century held that women were courting disaster when they did not give their all to the reproductive, domestic roles for which either God or nature had made them. Viewed within this larger context, Dr. Coleman's previously quoted warning—"Science pronounces that the woman who studies is lost!"—can be seen to be the medical rule, not the exception.

Considerations of the sort Van Evrie used to validate the natural inferiority of African Americans also played a role in defining women's place in nature's scheme of things. Nineteenth-century physiologists "proved" that the female brain was smaller than the brains of the most advanced humans— namely, white men. Synthesizing this and other scientific results, Carl Vogt, a professor of natural history, concluded that "the grown-up Negro partakes, as regards his intellectual faculties, of the nature of the child, the female, and the senile White" (in Ehrenreich and English 1978:106). Women—that is to say, *white* women—were found to be intellectually equal to *some* men— namely, grown-up Negroes and senile whites.

The perils women faced when they ventured out of their proper sphere and into the one reserved for grown-up, not-yet-senile white men was explained in terms of the sheer foolishness of acting contrary to nature and nature's God. It remained for men to protect women against themselves, which they were enjoined to do by both what the Bible taught and what the day's best science verified. To restrict women to the sphere for which both nature and God had prepared them—the home—was the least a responsible loving husband or father could do.

Homosexuality and Christianity: The Sin Model

Whereas those who have struggled to create a more inclusive moral community in America by championing the rights of African Americans and women can point to the passage of constitutional amendments that have advanced their cause, advocates for freedom and equality for gays and lesbians can make no comparable gesture. Indeed, as recently as 1986 the U.S. Supreme Court upheld a Georgia sodomy statute that criminalizes homosexual acts performed by consenting adults in the privacy of their own homes (Rubenstein 1993).

Homosexuality was criminalized on American soil even before there was an America. A 1636 Plymouth Colony law designates eight capital offenses, including "Treason . . . ; Willful murder; Solemn compaction or conversing with the devil . . . ; and Sodomy, rapes, buggery [and] Adultery" (in Rubenstein 1993::47–48). This law was revised in June 1671, when the number of capital offenses grew to sixteen with the addition of such crimes as "Blasphemy" and "Cursing or Smiting Mother or Father." The provision concerning sodomy reads as follows: "If any man lyeth with Mankind, as he lyeth with a Woman, both of them have committed Abomination; they both shall surely be put to Death, unless the one party were forced, or be under fourteen years of Age: And all other Sodomitical filthiness, shall surely be punished according to the nature of it" (in ibid.:52). This same statute is noteworthy because, in addition to including lesbianism, it also designates heterosexual anal intercourse and masturbation as crimes meriting the death penalty.

In 1697, when Plymouth Colony joined Massachusetts, the language of the law was changed, but not the punishment: men who were "duly convicted of lying with Mankind, as [they] lyeth with a woman . . . shall suffer the Pains of Death" (in Rubenstein 1993:52–53). And suffer they surely have. Both gays and lesbians have been drowned, hanged, choked, burned, and stoned to death for their "abomination." Witness this case from the Dutch New Netherlands Colony on Manhattan Island in 1646: "June 25. Court proceedings. Fiscal [public prosecutor] vs. Jan Creoli, a Negro, sodomy; second offense; this crime being condemned by God (Gen., c. 19; Levit., c. 18, 22, 29) as an abomination, the prisoner is sentenced to be conveyed to the place of public execution, and there choked to death, and then burnt to ashes" (in Katz 1976:22–23).

After the founding of the United States, a few progressives led by Jefferson thought death was too severe a punishment for men who engaged in homosexual behavior. Jefferson and his followers undertook the task of reforming Virginia law. The recommended change, which was never enacted, states: "Whosoever shall be guilty of Rape, Polygamy, or Sodomy with man or woman shall be punished, if a man, by castration, if a woman, by cutting thro' the cartilage of her nose a hole of half an inch in diameter at least" (in Katz 1976:24).

Obviously, even among America's early progressives, the punishment recommended for homosexual acts was anything but mild. Nevertheless, anyone seeking a reasonable defense for construing such acts between mutually consenting adults as a serious crime will find the voice of the Bible ringing throughout the land. And this is not an imaginary voice.

The execution of Jan Creoli, cited earlier, makes this clear in the case of America's earliest settlers. They believed that the Bible not only permitted but required death for the sin of sodomy. Among the most commonly cited biblical verses was Leviticus 20:13, which provided the text for the first Plymouth Colony sodomy law, including the death sentence. Leviticus 18:22–23 contains these words: "You shall not lie with a male as with a woman; it is an abomination. You shall not have sexual relations with any animal . . . ; it is perversion."

The biblical denunciation of homosexuality resonates across centuries. In 1810, for example, an indictment for attempted sodomy was issued in Baltimore County, Maryland; the accused was described as "not having the fear of God before his eyes, but being moved and seduced by the instigation's of the Devil" (in Greenberg 1988:355). Christians who today condemn homosexuality as both a sin against God and a violation of the criminal law (and evidence suggests that their number is not small) are an echo of America's past.

Before moving on to consider an alternative view of homosexuality, it is worth noting that human sexual relations with an animal (bestiality), an activity also criminalized in early America, were, like homosexual relations, punished by death. By way of example we have a 1662 case in New Haven, Connecticut, where a man named Potter, described as being "devout in worship, gifted in prayer, forward in edifying discourse among the religious, and zealous in reforming the sins of other people," was hanged for his offense, as were a steer, two heifers, three sheep, and two sows (Hyde 1916:708). In America punishment by death for the crime of bestiality persisted into the twentieth century.

Homosexuality and Science: The Sickness Model

During the second half of the nineteenth century, as psychiatry gained increasing acceptance as a science, a new model—the sickness model—took its place alongside the sin model as a way to understand homosexuality. Instead of being regarded as morally depraved people living in sin, homosexuals were now viewed as mentally ill and in need of professional medical help. The explanation of this illness depended on the theory that was favored. For example, behaviorists believed that homosexuality is a learned response and thus can be unlearned. Others, following Freud, located homosexuality's cause in traumatic childhood experiences that the person in need of treatment has repressed. Still others maintained that homosexuality results from chemical imbalances, especially in the brain.

Theoretical differences to one side, the sickness model brought about an important change in the way homosexuals were viewed. No longer regarded as persons to be morally blamed or punished by the state for acting on their sexual desires, homosexuals were now seen as individuals needing to be cured. In this case, however, *cured* tended to have a daunting meaning; usually it meant eliminating all sexual desires or replacing unnatural, abnormal homosexual desires with natural, normal heterosexual ones.

Some late nineteenth- and early twentieth-century psychiatrists tried to deal with homosexuals as the persons they were rather than change them into someone else; these therapists sought to help homosexuals move beyond their guilt and shame, which the therapists believed were caused by an uninformed, morally prejudiced culture, to a point where their patients could accept and even enjoy their sexual identities. These psychiatrists were a small minority among their scientific peers, however. The vast majority viewed their patients as mentally ill. For these physicians, the therapeutic challenge was to discover how best to cure them.

Attempting to meet this challenge involved exploring various therapies, including abstinence, hypnosis, psychoanalysis, vasectomy, shock treatment, the administration of hormones and drugs, castration (in the case of men), hysterectomy (in the case of women), lobotomy, and aversion therapies. The following case, from 1964, is illustrative of a type of aversion therapy called emetic aversion therapy because it involves the use of a drug that induces nausea and vomiting. "Aversion therapy was conducted on a male homosexual who had a heart condition. The particular form of aversion therapy involved creation of nausea, by means of an emetic, accompanied by talking about his homosexuality. The second part of the therapy involved recovery from the nausea and talking about pleasant ideas and heterosexual fantasies, which was sometimes aided by lysergic acid" (in Katz 1976:134). Almost as an afterthought, the psychiatrists who treated this patient add,

"In this case, the patient died as a result of a heart attack brought on by the use of the emetic."

Behaviorists favored aversion therapy; the aim was to create a new stimulus-response pattern, one that would replace homosexual responses with asexual or heterosexual ones. Freudians favored hypnosis and psychoanalysis, while those who believed that homosexuality results from a chemical imbalance experimented with a variety of drugs and shock therapy.

Whatever their theoretical allegiance, most psychiatrists found homosexuality so abhorrent that, as Chandler Burr remarks, "virtually any proposed treatment seemed defensible." By way of illustration, Burr notes the following.

> Lesbians were forced to submit to hysterectomies and estrogen injections, although it became clear that neither of these had any effect on sexual orientation. Gay men were subjected to similar abuses. *Changing Our Minds* [a 1992 documentary] incorporates a film clip from the late 1940s . . . of a young man undergoing a transorbital lobotomy. We see a small device like an ice pick inserted through the eye socket, above the eyeball and into the brain. The pick is moved back and forth, reducing the prefrontal lobe to a hemorrhaging pulp. [*Changing Our Minds*] also includes a grainy black-and-white clip from a 1950s educational film produced by the U.S. Navy. A gay man lies in a hospital bed. Doctors strap him down and attach electrodes to his head. "We're going to help you get better," says a male voice in the background. When the power is turned on, the body of the gay man jerks violently, and he begins to scream. (Burr 1993:48)

In addition to lobotomy, castration continued to be utilized well into the twentieth century, notwithstanding the lack of any serious scientific evidence supporting its therapeutic advantage.

As the twentieth century wore on, the number of dissidents within the psychiatric community grew, as did the incidence of public confrontations by gay rights activists. For example, at the 1970 meeting of the American Psychiatric Association, an activist disrupted a session by shouting: "You are the pigs who make it possible for the cops to beat homosexuals: they call us queer, you—so politely—call us sick. But it's the same thing. You make possible the beatings and rapes in prisons, you are implicated in the torturous cures perpetrated on desperate homosexuals" (in Conrad and Schneider 1992:204).

Finally, in 1974, bowing to criticisms both from its own members and the angry voices of the gay community, the American Psychiatric Association voted to exclude homosexuality from its list of mental illnesses in its *Diagnostic and Statistical Manual*. Instead, the 1974 *DSM* introduced the "Homosexual-Conflict Disorder," which it defined as follows:

> This category is for individuals whose sexual interests are directed primarily toward people of the same sex and who are either disturbed by, in conflict with, or wish to change their sexual orientation. This diagnostic category is distinguished from homosexuality which by itself does not necessarily constitute a psychiatric disorder. Homosexuality per se is one form of sexual behavior and, like other forms of sexual behavior, which are not by themselves psychiatric disorders, is not listed in this nomenclature of mental disorder. (in Conrad and Schneider 1992:208)

Most gay rights activists greeted this change as a victory. A few were skeptical. They noted the absence of an entry for "Heterosexual-Conflict Disorder." They also cited subsequent studies that revealed that a strong majority—about 70 percent—of psychiatrists continued to regard homosexuality as a "pathological adaptation" in response to which the medical goal was to reorient the patient toward the heterosexual paradigm (Conrad and Schneider 1992:208).

The same has been true of the medical profession generally. In 1981 the American Medical Association adopted a policy that recommended treating unhappy gays and lesbians by helping them change into happy heterosexuals. It was not until December 1994 that the AMA voted to encourage its members to adopt a "non judgmental [*sic*] recognition of sexual orientation."

How far America will move toward recognizing the rights of gays and lesbians—for example, granting gays and lesbians the same protections as others when it comes to employment, housing, marriage, parenting, and medical and tax benefits—remains to be seen. When antisodomy laws pass constitutional scrutiny, as they did in the 1986 case *Bowers v. Hardwick*, and when these laws are never enforced against those heterosexuals who violate them, it is difficult to imagine gays and lesbians winning full moral equality anytime soon. What is clear now is that the struggle to gain acceptance of gay men and lesbian women within the community of moral equals, like the struggle to gain acceptance of African Americans and women in general, has had to deal with some of the same powerful sources of resistance, widespread religious and scientific opinion in particular. The same is no less true of a contemporary challenge to the moral status quo, one that, if anything, is an even greater challenge than the others discussed to this point.

A Contemporary Variation on the Main Themes

For many Americans, probably even the majority, the idea of including animals in the community of moral equals is a nonstarter. Granted, we should never be sadistically cruel to animals. Granted, we should encourage kindness to them. But this is as far as it goes. We do nothing wrong when we eat them, wear their hides or skins, hunt and trap them for recreation or profit, train them to perform tricks we find amusing, exhibit them in zoos or aquariums, or use them as tools in education, product testing, and medical research. Of course, using *human beings* in these ways would be wrong, but none of this is wrong in the case of animals. Humans are all members of the moral community; other animals, because they are inferior and thus unequal to us, are not.

There is an already large, steadily growing body of philosophical and legal literature devoted to the debate about animal rights (Magel 1989). Canvassing this literature is not my interest here. Instead, I want to sketch the broad outlines of the religious and scientific resistance to the idea that nonhuman animals should be included in the moral community.

Animals: The Biblical Basis for Exclusion

For most Christians, the biblical basis for excluding nonhuman animals is there from the beginning, both in Genesis's account of God's activities on the sixth day of creation and in God's blessing of Noah and his sons after the deluge. Here, first, is the description of the sixth day.

> And God said, "Let the earth bring forth living creatures according to their kind: cattle and creeping things and beasts of the earth according to their kind." And it was so.
>
> And God made the beasts of the earth according to their kind, and everything that creeps upon the ground according to its kind. And God saw that it was good. Then God said, "Let us make man in our image, after our likeness; and let them have dominion over the fish of the sea, and over the birds of the air, and over the cattle, and over all the earth, and over every creeping thing that creeps upon the earth." So God created man in his own image, in the image of God he created him: male and female he created them. And God blessed them, and God said to them, "Be fruitful and multiply, and fill the earth and subdue it; and have dominion over the fish of the sea and over the birds of the air and over every living thing that moves upon the earth." . . . And God saw everything that he had made, and behold, it was very good. (Gen. 1:24–28, 31a)

Concerning God's blessing, we read the following.

> And God blessed Noah and his sons, and said to them, "Be fruitful and multiply, and fill the earth. The fear of you and the dread of you shall be upon every beast of the earth, and upon every bird of the air, upon everything that creeps upon the ground and all the fish of the sea; into your hands they are delivered. Every living thing that lives shall be food for you; and as I gave you the green plants, I give you everything. Only you shall not eat life with its life, that is, its blood." (Gen. 9:1–4)

This latter selection from Genesis concerns what God gives us to eat. The message seems clear: it is not just "green plants," not just our "veggies"; it is "everything." In his *Commentaries on the First Book of Moses called Genesis,* John Calvin speaks for the dominant Christian view when he insists that "we must firmly retain the liberty given us by the Lord. . . . For it is an insuperable tyranny, when God, the Creator of all things, has laid open to us the earth and the air, in order that we may thence take food as from his storehouse, for these to be shut up from us by mortal man, who is not even able to create a snail or a fly" (Calvin 1847:293).

The "mortal man" Calvin has in mind, the one who would exercise "insuperable tyranny" by proscribing some foods God has given to us, is the vegetarian. "I assert," Calvin declares, "that atrocious injury is done to God, when we give such license to men [i.e., vegetarians] as to allow them to pronounce that unlawful which God designs to be lawful, and to bind consciences which the word of God sets free, with their fictitious laws" (1847:293).

Christians have insisted on more, however, than just our God-given right to consume animals as food. In the case of animal experimentation, Cannon John McCarthy speaks for the dominant Christian view when he writes:

> Experimentation on living animals, even though they may suffer severe pain in the process, is lawful to the extent that it is necessary for a genuine scientific purpose which may benefit humanity. It is unlawful to inflict any unnecessary suffering on animals either in the course of vivisection experiments or otherwise. . . . It is a question of fact whether unnecessary suffering is sometimes inflicted in vivisection experiments. There may, indeed, be such abuses. If so, they are regrettable and should be eradicated. But we cannot condemn vivisection *in toto* because of abuses accidentally associated with it. (McCarthy 1960:156)

Why are we barred from doing this—from condemning vivisection in toto? Canon McCarthy answers by reminding his readers that "in God's arrangement, animals are created to serve human needs" (1960:156).

And as for hunting—to take just one final example—Pastor William H. Ammon, executive director of Sportsmen for Christ, writes: "It's not hard to know what God expects, if you know your Bible. The Bible never changes, because God never changes. What He hated thousands of years ago, He hates today. What he loved then, He loves now. It certainly makes things easier for us, doesn't it?" (Ammon 1989:62).

In the particular case of hunting, Pastor Ammon believes he knows God's mind. "God's attitude about hunting hasn't changed," he insists. "I can read how He reacted in the past and know everything still holds true today. I know that God set this world up so man could sustain his life as he replenished the earth. Whether man was killing a sacrificial animal or game that God provided in the field, it was all part of God's system. There are no anti-hunting slogans in the Bible" (1989:62). For those Christian hunters who are successful and "collect game," Ammon observes, "Congratulations will be in order: We'll know they did so because they could handle their weapons, their flesh, and their spirits. They were fair, they played by the rules and prayed by the rules; theirs will be the victory of faith that prevailed. . . . At home, Mom and the kids will be excited because Dad has gone with God on the hunt" (79).

Animals: The Scientific Basis for Exclusion

Our culture's widespread belief in the inferiority of nonhuman animals and their exclusion from the community of moral equals has not lacked for scientists willing to offer their support, in the name of science, to what religious people have accepted as a matter of revealed faith. This scientific defense has taken two forms. On the one hand, legions of scientists have offered proofs of the intellectual and rational inferiority of nonhuman animals compared to humans. On the other hand, humans who have raised their voices in favor of human and animal equality have been subjected to ad hominem vilification; some scientists have even gone so far as to claim that people who care deeply about the way animals are treated are mentally ill. I will return to this second form of defense below. First, though, there is the matter of animal intelligence, or the lack thereof.

This belief has deep roots in Greek thought. When Aristotle defined man as a "rational animal," standing above all other animals in the hierarchy of value, he was echoing the ideas of his teacher, Plato, just as Plato was echoing those of his predecessors. Some scientists, following Descartes, went further: they denied not only that animals are rational or intelligent but also that animals are aware of anything, including pain. Burn, drown, starve, or slice open an animal without the benefit of anesthetic, and the result is always and everywhere the same: the animal is not aware of anything.

This was a convenient belief for seventeenth-century Cartesian scientists since it absolved them of any moral qualms when they vivisected animals. Nicholas Fontaine offers this chilling eye-witness description of the activities of French vivisectors under Descartes's influence at Port Royal: "The [Cartesian] scientists administered beatings to dogs with perfect indifference and made fun of those who pitied the creatures as if they felt pain. They said the animals were clocks; that the cries they emitted when struck were only the noise of a little spring that had been touched, but that the whole body was without feeling. They nailed the poor animals up on boards by their four paws to vivisect them to see the circulation of the blood which was a great subject of controversy" (in Rosenfield 1968:54).

The Cartesian scientists clearly did not view nonhuman animals as having a moral status equal to our own. Regarding what was done to these animals, Descartes's followers failed to see that there was any moral question to be raised. Remarkably, even today some respected scientists actively keep this aspect of Cartesianism alive and well. Writing in a 1971 issue of *The American Scholar*, for example, Robert J. White, a professor of surgery at Case Western Reserve University whose research has included attempted transplants of brains from one primate to another, declares that "the inclusion of lower animals in our ethical system is philosophically meaningless" (1976:169). Not one to alter his core beliefs easily, Professor White, this time writing in a 1990 *Hastings Center Report* that included a special supplement on ethical questions relating to research on nonhuman animals, reaffirms his disapproval. "I am extremely disappointed in this particular series of articles, which, quite frankly, has no right to be published as part of the *Report*. Animal usage is not a moral or ethical issue and elevating the problem of animal rights to such a plane is a disservice to medical research and the farm and dairy industry" (White 1990:43).

White is hardly alone among prestigious researchers in not seeing animal rights as a moral or ethical issue. Noble laureate David Baltimore was among a group of panelists who took part in a discussion of Fred Wiseman's 1974 documentary *Primates*, as was the Harvard moral philosopher Robert Nozick. During the discussion, entitled *The Price of Knowledge*, which aired on WNET-TV on September 12, 1975, Nozick states that "animals used in research count for something themselves"; he then asks Baltimore whether he thinks the isolation, pain, and death experienced by animals in laboratories have "a moral cost."

> Baltimore: Well, I think I'd answer no. Gratuitous killing of animals has been going on for centuries; hunting, that kind of thing.
> Nozick: But we would condemn that, wouldn't we? . . . Have we ever heard people saying, there are these experiments that can be done on animals, but . . . though we'll learn something, it wouldn't be important enough to justify killing . . . five hundred animals[?] Has that ever occurred in the scientific community?
> Baltimore: I don't think it really is a moral question. It's a question of, here we sit, we want to survive, [and] we get some pleasure out of it.

Early America did not prove to be fertile ground for Cartesianism. The world's first animal protection legislation dates from the "Body of Liberties" adopted by the Massachusetts Bay Colony in 1641. Section 91 states "That no man shall exercise any tyranny or cruelty toward any brute creatures which are usually kept for the use of man" (in Finsen and Finsen 1994:42). For America, including American scientists, the central historical question has not been whether animals can feel pain but how humans can be justified in causing it.

In the particular case of animal experimentation, some scientists have offered justifications based on the intrinsic value of the knowledge obtained. A justification of this type, however, invites an obvious response: if the knowledge obtained justifies the pain caused in obtaining it, then knowledge gained from research on *human* subjects also seems to be justified.

Some scientists have been willing to accept this implication. The twentieth century American chemist E. E. Slosson writes that "a human life is nothing compared with a new fact. . . . the aim of science is the advancement of human knowledge at any sacrifice of human life" (in Vyvyan 1989:20–21). Most American scientists, however, have sought a justification of animal experimentation in particular and human exploitation of nonhuman animals in general that would position humans and other animals in two quite different moral spheres.

Among the possible objective grounds that have been offered in this regard are (1) that humans are unique in being able to use tools; (2) that humans are unique in being able to use language; and (3) that humans are unique in being able to pass on the knowledge accumulated by one generation to future generations. Proponents of these ideas have claimed that they are demonstrable, objective facts about the world, not truths that rest on religious faith. Moreover, proponents have argued that these objective facts prove that a qualitative difference separates humans from other animals. This qualitative difference thus provides the scientific basis for admitting only humans to the community of moral equals.

Not all humans have agreed. Some critics have challenged the various assertions of human uniqueness. They have argued that chimpanzees are able to use tools (as when they insert twigs into termite mounds and then eat the termites that cling to the twigs); that chimpanzees, dolphins, and other animals have demonstrated their capacity to use language; and that Japanese macaques have passed on the culture of "potato washing" from one generation to the next.

Other critics have taken a different route. Even though humans and other animals may differ in what they can do (use tools, master a language, etc.), these critics deny that these are morally relevant differences. After all, we do not accept the premise that we can eat or vivisect human beings who are unable to use tools, participate in the acquisition of transgenerational knowledge, and the like. It is a matter of prejudice, not rational principle, these critics contend, that explains why nonhuman animals are excluded from the community of moral equals.

Such challenges do not sit well with many people who have a vested interest in retaining the moral status quo. This has proven to be especially true of scientists with ties to the agricultural, hunting, trapping, and animal-research communities, for example. These are the arenas where many scientists have had recourse to the second form of defense mentioned earlier: ad hominem attacks.

As is true of the animal rights movement today, women were the majority voice raised against vivisection during the nineteenth century. Not surprisingly, given the then dominant ideology of the two spheres, these women were characterized as "silly women led astray," a "swarm of buzzing idlers," and criticized for failing to discharge their proper duties in the home because of their excessive "sentimentality" (Anon. 1885).

What could explain why so many women would "bray persistent" against researchers who had dedicated their lives to discovering nature's "hidden gifts of cure"? The French physiologist Elie de Cyon had an answer. "Is it necessary to repeat that women—rather—old maids—form the most numerous contingent of [our critics]? Let my adversaries contradict me, if they can show me among the leaders of the agitation one girl, rich, beautiful, and beloved, or some young wife, who has found in her home the full satisfaction of her affections?" (de Cyon 1883:506). In other words, in their compassion for animals, these women betrayed their frustration at not being cared for themselves—by men, that is.

Elie de Cyon's language, though certainly offensive, is of a piece with the rhetoric of derision many scientists practice today. People who are committed to ending the exclusion of nonhuman animals from the moral community are regularly attacked as "ignorant," "emotional," "illogical," "antirational," "antiscientific," and "antihuman." Collectively, these same people are represented as "fanatics," "extremists," and "terrorists." Public expressions of doubts about their mental stability are not uncommon, as the following passage, again from neurosurgeon Robert J. White, illustrates: "As a concerned scientist and practicing neurosurgeon, I am simply unable to plumb the depths of a philosophy that places such a premium on animal life even at the expense of human existence and improvement. It would appear that this preoccupation with the alleged pain and suffering of the animals used in medical research may well represent, at the very least, social prejudice against medicine or, more seriously, true psychiatric aberrations" (1976:169).

White is neither the first nor the last scientist to have raised doubts about the psychological fitness of critics of vivisection. The author of a 1909 essay in *Science* magazine wrote that because "antagonism to vivisection is a form of incurable insanity, those who suffer from it are wholly indifferent to argument or facts, and their delusional convictions urge them irresistibly to constant repetition of the same mad acts" (in Buettinger 1993:281). In other words, antivivisectionists suffer from a form of obsessive insanity.

As it happens, this was the diagnosis reached by the American neurologist Charles Loomis Dana. He even gave the newly discovered psychosis a name: *zoophil-psychosis* (literally, "love of animals psychosis"). Dana's discovery was heralded in the *New York Times*. "Passion for Animals Really a Disease," the headline blared. Dana's patients included a man who did not like to see horses "checked up, or whipped, or docked, or driven fast" and a woman who "could not bear to have a cat suffer. She made her home a hospital for stray cats . . . [Her husband's] life was made utterly wretched by this condition of affairs" (in Buettinger 1993:283).

Dana's medicalization of deeply felt empathy for animal suffering as a psychotic disorder was enthusiastically adopted by the vivisection community. As the contemporary American historian Craig Buettinger remarks, "Dana claimed antivivisection sentiment sprang from flaws of the female mind and a mental malfunction in some males. For the vivisectionists of Dana's day, his diagnosis was the preferred way to characterize the opposition" (1993:288). Moreover, as Buettinger goes on to note, Dana's ideology of insanity survived even as late as the 1960s, when the American scientist Clarence Dennis voiced his opposition to passage of the 1966 Animal Welfare Act by reiterating the charge of zoophil-psychosis against the act's proponents (Dennis 1966:832). What Buettinger fails to mention is how, despite the scientific community's abandonment of Dana's diagnosis, scientists such as Dr. White still raise doubts about the "true psychiatric aberrations" of those who demand extending to nonhuman animals the same relevant protections extended to human beings, and why even today many scientific defenders of the moral status quo evidently believe that a rational, logical, scientific way to respond to their critics is to call them bad names—"misanthropes," "fanatics," "extremists," and "terrorists."

Moral Time Travel

My object here has not been to attempt to prove any partisan's views right or wrong. This is the customary posture of the philosopher, and if the truth be told, I do not feel entirely comfortable in having assumed a different one. Nevertheless, having come this far in my uncertain odyssey on this mysterious, wondrous planet, I think I understand that philosophy plants no deep roots in people if it is reduced to a contest between competing ideas. I do not mean to suggest, and I do not believe, that a fully developed human being can avoid testing the truth and logic of ideas, which is one way to understand both what philosophy is and what it demands of us. I mean only that the mere spectacle of the clash of competing ideas needs a larger context if it is to have a meaning in our lives. But that is another story best reserved for some other venue.

One thing my survey of relevant American history shows is that religious belief and scientific doctrine, often represented as antagonistic to each other, can collude in defense of the moral status quo. When slaves from Africa, women, and gays and lesbians were denied rights and privileges accorded to (some) white men, the logic of exclusion found both a Christian and a scientific voice. Belief was far from unanimous. Many Christians and scientists disputed the logic of exclusion canvassed here. Indeed, I think it is safe to say that without the efforts of people of faith, whatever that faith might be, and of those Americans committed to the scientific enterprise, it is unlikely that America's original, dominant conception of the moral community would have evolved into a more inclusive one. Still, the other side of the story—the side I have emphasized on this occasion—is the side of Christian and scientific resistance to any change in the moral status quo. This frequently neglected side of the story is one we need to know if we are to understand what it is to be an American.

For many of us, I imagine, it is difficult to take some of the biblical and scientific arguments seriously. But this we know: many people did (and many still do) take these ideas seriously; indeed, many Americans lived their lives the way they did, and many continue to live their lives the way they do, *because* these ideas were or are taken seriously. It is no merely academic matter, I think, to accept these facts and try to make sense of them in our own lives.

When I do this, I wonder what I would have believed and done if I had lived in the times of the Plymouth Colony; of Washington, Jefferson, and Lincoln; of Rev. Armstrong and Jupiter Hammon; of Dr. Van Evrie, Thomas Dew, and Orestes Brownson; or of Drs. Coleman, Clark, Hall, and Vogt; or been part of the twentieth-century debate among psychiatrists and other physicians concerning whether homosexuality is a disease. Would I have been among the majority who invoked God's word or the findings of an objective science to defend excluding blacks, women, gays, and lesbians from the community of moral equals, or would I have been among the minority who called for including them?

I play this question over and over again in my imagination. I know what I want to believe. I want to believe that I would have been one of those who agitated for change in the moral status quo—the minority who saw through the flimsy fabric of prejudice, ignorance, custom, and fear that barred acceptance of all humans as moral equals, each to all.

Whether I would have been an agitator or an acceptor, I do not know. The power that the dominant culture into which we are born exercises over our ability to think independently is great; our will to think on our own is small. Perhaps I would have been counted among the majority and defended to my dying breath the divinely sanctified and scientifically confirmed reasons for thinking that blacks and women are inferior to white men and that gays and lesbians either live in sin or are sick. Who is to say what any of us would have thought and done in times and circumstances that in some ways are so different from our own?

Perhaps one way we can enter imaginatively into the murky past is to force ourselves to come to terms with the present. And perhaps one way we can do this is to ask ourselves how much our will to think on our own shuts down when we confront the idea of including nonhuman animals in the moral community. How we respond to this question, here and now, I think, may be the closest thing we know, firsthand, that is experientially comparable to how our predecessors thought whether to accept blacks or women, for example, as equal members.

Seriously to ask about the moral equality of animals other than the human is no ivory tower question. If we were to grant nonhuman animals equal moral status, we would be obliged to reconstruct our conception of who we and they are, and we would also be obliged to change how they are treated. No longer could we suppose that we may use them simply for our benefit, either because "that's why God made them" or because "human superiority can be demonstrated by an objective science." No longer could we suppose that they exist so that we might eat them, or wear their hides or skins, or use them as tools in education, product testing, research, and so on. On the contrary, we would be obliged to put an end to these and many other exploitive practices.

For my part—and I do not say that this must be true of everyone, only that it is true in my own case—I think that how I respond to the question of whether nonhuman animals should be included as equal members of the ideal moral community is a useful litmus test suggesting what I would have thought and done in the past, when the demands for freedom and equality were heard in America on behalf of members of other traditionally excluded groups, Native and African Americans, women, and gays and lesbians among them.

I suspect that if today I do not recognize the merits of the question about enfranchising nonhuman animals into the moral community, then neither would I have recognized the merits of the demand to think about including the humans I have just mentioned, whereas if I am alive and responsive to the former idea, then I believe I might have been alive and responsive to the others.

Perhaps I am mistaken. Moral time travel ("What would we have thought and done if we had been born and lived in the past?") of necessity explores uncharted moral terrain. The best we can do is transport our existing moral sense imaginatively back in time, mindful that, whatever moral prejudices we find, people of faith and practitioners of science will be there to assure us that the then existing moral arrangements are the right ones, just as, flesh and blood as we are, stationed here in the world today, this same assurance is offered by many people who speak these same languages.

Works Cited

Ammon, William H. 1989. *The Christian Hunter's Guide to Survival.* Old Tappen, N.J.: Fleming H. Revell.

Anon. 1885. "Somnia Medici." *Zoophilist,* May 1.

Armstrong, George D. 1969 [1857]. *The Christian Doctrine of Slavery.* New York: Negro Universities Press.

Brownson, Orestes A. 1885 [1873]. "The Woman Question. Article II." In *The Works of Orestes A. Brownson,* 20 vols., ed. Henry F. Brownson, 18:398–417. Detroit, Mich.: H. F. Brownson.

———. 1905 [1869]. "The Woman Question. Article I." In *The Works of Orestes A. Brownson,* ed. Henry F. Brownson, vols., 18:381–97. Detroit, Mich.: H. F. Brownson.

Buettinger, Craig. 1993. "Antivivisection and the Charge of Zoophil-Psychosis in the Early Twentieth Century." *The Historian* 55, no. 2:277–88.

Burr, Chandler. 1993. "Homosexuality and Biology." *Atlantic Monthly,* March, pp. 47–61.

Calvin, John. 1847. *Commentaries on the First Book of Moses called Genesis,* vol. 1. Ed. John King. Edinburgh: Calvin Translation Society.

Conrad, Peter, and Joseph W. Schneider. 1992. *Deviance and Medicialization: From Badness to Sickness.* Philadelphia: Temple University Press.

de Cyon, Elie. 1883. "The Anti-Vivisection Agitation." *Contemporary Review* 43 (Apr.): 498–516.

Dennis, Clarence. 1966. "America's Littlewood Crisis: The Sentimental Threat to Animal Research." *Surgery* 60 (Oct.): 827–39.

Dew, Thomas R. 1835. "Dissertation on the Characteristic Differences between the Sexes, and the Position and Influence of Woman in Society." *Southern Literary Messenger,* May, pp. 493–512, 621–32, 672–91.

Ehrenreich, Barbara, and Dierdre English. 1978. *For Her Own Good: 150 Years of Experts' Advice to Women.* New York: Doubleday.

Finsen, Lawrence, and Susan Finsen. 1994. *The Animal Rights Movement in America: From Compassion to Respect.* New York: Twayne.

Greenberg, David F. 1988. *The Construction of Homosexuality.* Chicago: University of Chicago Press.

Gould, Stephen Jay. 1981. *The Mismeasure of Man.* New York: W. W. Norton.

Hammon, Jupiter. 1787. *An Address to the Negroes of the State of New York.* New York: African Society. Excerpts in *Slavery: Opposing Viewpoints,* ed. William Dudley. San Diego, Calif.: Greenhaven, 1992. Page references are to the latter edition.

Hyde, Walter Woodburn. 1916. "The Prosecution and Punishment of Animals and Lifeless Things in the Middle Ages and Modern Times." *University of Pennsylvania Law Review* 64:696–730.

Katz, Jonathan. 1976. *Gay American History: Lesbians and Gay Men in the U.S.A.* New York: Thomas Y. Crowell.

Landrine, Hope. 1988. "Revising the Framework of Abnormal Psychology." In *Teaching a Psychology of People: Resources for Gender and Sociocultural Awareness,* ed. Phyllis Bronstein and Kathyrn Quina, 37–44. Washington, D.C.: American Psychological Association.

Lincoln, Abraham. 1906. "Address on Colonization to a Deputation of Colored Men. In *The Writings of Abraham Lincoln*, 8 vols., ed. Arthur Brooks Lapsley, vol. 6, 1862–63, pp. 113–120. New York: Putnam's.

Magel, Charles. 1989. *Keyguide to Information Sources in Animal Rights*. Jefferson, N.C.: McFarland.

McCarthy, Canon John. 1960. *Problems in Theology*, vol. 2: *The Commandments*. Dublin: Browne and Noland.

Nie, Judith. 1977. *Seven Women: Portraits from the American Radical Tradition*. New York: Penguin Books.

Rosenfield, Leonora. 1968. *From Beast-Machine to Man-Machine*. New York: Columbia University Press.

Rubenstein, William B., ed. 1993. *Lesbians, Gay Men, and the Law*. New York: New Press.

Van Evrie, J. H. 1868. *White Supremacy and Negro Subordination: or, Negroes a Subordinate Race, and (so-called) Slavery Its Normal Condition*. 2d ed. New York: Van Evrie, Horton.

Vyvyan, John. 1989. *The Dark Face of Science*. Marblehead, Mass.: Micah.

White, Robert J. 1976 [1971]. "Antivivisection: The Reluctant Hydra." In *Animal Rights and Human Obligations*, ed. Tom Regan and Peter Singer, 163–69. Englewood Cliffs, N.J.: Prentice-Hall.

———. 1990. *Hastings Center Report* 20 (Nov.–Dec.): 43.

7

UNDERSTANDING ANIMAL RIGHTS VIOLENCE

Few issues divide animal rights advocates more than the role violence should play in forwarding their objectives. Moreover, few matters unite opponents of animal rights more than the condemnation of the violence some attribute indiscriminately to all animal rights advocates. Whether advocate or opponent, one thing is clear: when it comes to discussions of animal rights and violence, there is a lot more heat than light.

Three important questions need to be distinguished. The first asks what violence is; the second, whether and, if so, when violence can be morally justified; and the third, why people use it. Concerning the first question, many animal rights advocates maintain that violence can be directed only against sentient forms of life, human and otherwise. As long as no one is hurt, no violence is done. Given this way of understanding violence, advocates who destroy only property—say, firebombing laboratories on university campuses or sinking pirate whaling ships on the high seas—can describe themselves as being engaged in nonviolent activism.

I do not think the concept of violence is limited in this way. Someone who sets fire to a vacant abortion clinic or torches an empty church causes no physical injury to any sentient being, but to suppose that these acts of arson are nonviolent seems to me badly to distort what *violence* means. We do not need to hurt someone to use violence against something. To the extent that animal rights advocates engage in activities that damage or destroy property, they engage in violence.

Part of the reason some advocates define violence as they do can be traced to the way they answer the second question. Most advocates are pacifists; that is, most believe that violence is wrong. Because some of those advocates who view themselves as pacifists do not think it is wrong to blow up trucks loaded with furs or meat, the definition of violence is tailored to fit the demands of pacifism. All violence is wrong; since blowing up a truck is not wrong, it must not be violent.

The truth of the matter, I think, is different. If someone blows up a truck, torches a lab, or sinks an illegal whaling vessel, they do serious violence even if no one is hurt. To describe these acts as "nonviolent" is to misdescribe them, the way the military does when it describes civilians who are killed or maimed as "collateral damage." Nonetheless, the fact that the destruction of property counts as violence does not by itself make such destruction wrong. Whether the act is wrong remains an open question, one that cannot be answered merely by appealing to what words mean. No other moral question can be answered in this way. There is no reason to think that asking about the morality of violence should be answered any differently.

Of the three questions distinguished previously, it is the third one (the one that asks why animal advocates use violence) that I explore in the following pages. Near the end, however, I offer some suggestions concerning steps that could be taken to reduce the amount of violence committed in the name of animal rights. What violence is, and when, if ever, violence against property or sentient forms of life is morally justified are questions left for possible exploration on some future occasion.

"Understanding Animal Rights Violence" was originally presented at a 1993 meeting sponsored by the organization Public Responsibility in Medicine and Research Science in the Public Interest. It has not been previously published.

Those people who view themselves as advocates of animal rights—and I certainly include myself among them—also see themselves as part of a social justice movement: the animal rights movement. In this respect, animal rights advocates believe that common bonds unite them with those who have worked for justice in other quarters: for example, for women, people of color, the poor, and gays and lesbians. The struggle for equal rights for and among these people is hardly complete; the struggle for the rights of animals has only begun, and this latter struggle promises to be, if anything, more difficult and protracted than any of its social justice relatives. For while demands for equal rights for many historically disfranchised people face formidable obstacles, they have one advantage over the struggle for animal rights. None of the other movements I have mentioned challenges the conception of the moral community that has dominated Western thought and traditions, the one that includes *humans only*; rather, all these struggles work with rather than against this conception, demanding only (and I do not mean to minimize the enormous difficulties such a demand inevitably faces) that the boundaries of the moral community expand to include previously excluded human beings—Native Americans, for example, or humans who suffer from various physical or mental disabilities.

The struggle for animal rights is different; it calls for a deeper, more fundamental change in the way we think about membership in the moral community. It demands not an expansion but a dismantling of the for-humans-only conception, to be replaced by one that includes other-than-human animals.

Not surprisingly, therefore, any obstacle that stands in the way of greater justice for people of color or the poor, for example, also stands in the way of greater justice for chimpanzees and chickens, whereas the struggle for justice for chimpanzees and chickens encounters obstacles at once more fundamental and unique, including the resistance or disdain of people who are among the most enlightened when it comes to injustice done to humans. Any doubt about this can be readily dispelled by gauging the indifference and hostility showered on the very idea of animal rights by both many of the leaders and most of the rank and file in any human rights movement, including, for example, those committed to justice and equality for women and racial minorities.

Despite these differences, those of us involved in the struggle for animal rights need to remember that we share many of the challenges other social justice movements face. How these movements respond to these challenges, therefore, is something worthy of our study, something from which we can learn. But this is a subject for another occasion. Here, a related set of questions takes pride of place. These concern not external obstacles to social justice movements but internal divisions within them. By way of illustration, I want to explore a few of the similarities between the nineteenth-century antislavery movement in America and today's animal rights movement.

Before doing this, I want to try to defuse a possible misunderstanding. I am not in any way suggesting that the animal rights movement and the antislavery movement are in every respect the same (clearly, they are not), any more than I would be suggesting that all African Americans must be either gay or lesbian because there are similarities between the movement to liberate slaves, on the one hand, and the gay and lesbian movement, on the other. Similarities are just that: similarities. And one thing similarities are not is sameness.

Nevertheless, attending to the similarities I have in mind is not idle. A clearer understanding of the ideology of the antislavery movement and an appreciation of that movement's internal divisions can help us better understand the animal rights movement. In particular, understanding disagreements about the role of violence in the former can help us better understand debates about its role in the latter—or so I believe and hope to be able to explain. First, however, some stage setting regarding the idea of animal rights is in order.

Animal Rights versus Animal Welfare

When it comes to what we humans are morally permitted to do to other animals, it is safe to say that opinion is divided. Some people (abolitionists) believe that we should stop using nonhuman animals, whether as sources of food, as trained performers, or as models of various diseases, for example. Others (welfarists) think such utilization is permissible as long as it is done humanely. Those who accept the former outlook object to such utilization in principle and believe it should end in practice. Those who accept the latter outlook accept such utilization in principle and believe it may continue in practice, provided the welfare of animals is not unduly compromised, in which case these practices will need to be appropriately reformed. Clearly real differences separate these two ways of thinking, one abolitionist at its core, the other not. Anyone who would deny or attempt to minimize these differences would distort rather than describe the truth.

Language users that we are, we have a shared need for intelligible verbal markers, some word or phrase that captures and conveys these differences. It is against this larger background of philosophical disagreement and linguistic need that the expressions "animal rights" and "animal rights movement," on the one hand, and "animal welfare" and "animal welfare movement," on the other, have been introduced, with the former pair of expressions commonly used to refer to the abolitionist and the latter pair, to the reformist.

Language is an imperfect instrument, of course, and for all I know there may be better words to mark the differences at hand. I do not care what words we use. What I do care about is (1) the plain truth that such differences exist and (2) our willingness to acknowledge the existence of these differences honestly and forthrightly rather than to pretend or suggest that "it's all a matter of words," that "it really doesn't matter what we say, since it all comes to the same thing." That not only is not true; among people who know better, it is not honest.

One area where these differences can make a difference is the particular matter before us. For it is among abolitionists, not reformists—among animal rightists, not animal welfarists—that we find those willing to commit acts of violence in the name of animal liberation. Nevertheless—and this is of great importance—not all animal rightists are prepared to go this far. That is, within the animal rights movement one finds deep, protracted, principled disagreements about the limits of protest in general and the permissibility of using violence in particular.

Analogous ideological and tactical themes are to be found in the antislavery movement. That movement was anything but monolithic. True, all abolitionists shared a common goal: slavery in America had to end. Beyond their agreement concerning this unifying goal, however, partisans of emancipation divided over a rich, complex fabric of well-considered, passionately espoused, and irreconcilable disagreements concerning the appropriate means of ending it. For my purposes, reference to just three areas of disagreement will suffice.

Abolition First versus Abolition Later

Following the lead of William Lloyd Garrison (1831), some abolitionists called for the unconditional emancipation of slaves, insisting as well that former slave owners not receive compensation for their financial losses. "Immediatists" (as they were called) wanted to end slavery first and then go forward with various plans to educate and in other ways prepare the newly freed slaves for the responsibilities of full citizenship. Other abolitionists (Channing 1835) favored a "gradualist" approach: complete emancipation was the eventual goal, but only after various alternatives to slave labor and improvements in the life of the slaves were in place. Thus, some gradualists sought freedom for slaves after (not before) those in bondage had received at least a rudimentary education or acquired a marketable skill or after (not before) a plan of financial compensation to former slave owners, or another plan calling for voluntary recolonization, had been implemented.

To any and all such proposals, Garrison spoke for his fellow immediatists, declaring that gradualist steps would have opponents of slavery accept the moral absurdity of tolerating the very thing they opposed as a means to ending it. For immediatists, any proposal that required the continued bondage of some slaves today as the price of emancipating others tomorrow was morally unacceptable because it violated a higher moral law: the law that we are not to do evil that good may come.

This split between slavery's immediatists and gradualists is mirrored in today's animal rights movement. Some people who profess belief in the movement's abolitionist goals also believe that these goals can be achieved by using gradualist means—for example, by supporting protocols that aim to reduce or refine animal use in a scientific setting, with replacement possibly achieved later on, or by decreasing the number of hens raised in cages today as a step along the way to emptying cages tomorrow. In this way, it is believed, we can succeed both in making the lives of some animals better today and in ending all animal exploitation in the future.

Other animal rights abolitionists are cut from more Garrison-like cloth. For these animal rightists, *how* we get to the abolitionist goal, not just *that* we get there, matters morally (Francione and Regan 1992). Following the higher moral law that we are not to do evil that good may come, these activists believe that they should not tacitly support violating the rights of some animals today in the hope of freeing others tomorrow. For these activists, as was true of their counterparts in the antislavery movement, it is not a question of first finding an alternative to the evil being done before deciding whether to stop doing it; instead, one must first decide to end the evil and then look for another way to achieve the goals one seeks. For these animal rights activists, then, our first obligation is to stop using animals as we do; after we have satisfied this obligation, there will be plenty of time to search for alternative ways of doing what it is we want to do. To end evil now rather than later is what conformity to the higher moral law requires.

Working with the Government versus Working Independently

A second common theme concerns the role of government. The antislavery movement once again was sharply divided. Whereas Garrison and his followers refused to cooperate with the government, others insisted on the necessity of working with elected representatives; among this latter group, Frederick Douglass was unquestionably the most illustrious representative (see Douglass 1845).

This split between Garrison, Douglass, and their followers was not whimsical. It turned on alternative, well-considered readings of the Constitution of the United States. Garrison read the Constitution as a proslavery document. To see why, recall that blacks are therein counted as three-fifths persons; that, although the international slave trade was to end by 1808, no mention is made of freeing any of those slaves already in America; and that many of the framers of the constitution themselves owned slaves (Washington and Jefferson, in whose memory and honor impressive monuments stand in our nation's capital, were among the young nation's slave owners). To free the slaves, Garrison argued, it was first necessary to dissolve the Union.

Douglass, who for a time agreed with Garrison's position, not only reached a point where he read the Constitution differently; more important, he was prepared to act differently (Foner 1950:136–415). Whereas Garrison insisted that the Constitution was a proslavery document, a fact that made the American government itself morally unwarranted, Douglass added his power and influence to preserving the Union (for example, by recruiting two regiments of free blacks to fight in the Union Army during the Civil War). For Douglass, slavery would be and could be ended only by the federal government's use of military might and the power of law.

The Constitution contains no ambiguous language concerning nonhuman animals that might occasion a split among today's animal rights advocates like that between Garrison and Douglass. Cows and pigs, chimpanzees and dolphins, ospreys and squirrels—all are total nonpersons as far as the Constitution is concerned. Even so, what we might term the *political sensibilities* of Garrison and Douglass live on in today's animal rights movement.

Douglass's faith in the role of government is represented by those animal rights advocates who look to the government—laws, enforcement mechanisms, and the courts—as essential elements in realizing the abolitionist goal for which they labor. In contrast, Garrison's disdain for the government is mirrored by today's animal rights activists who have lost faith in the progressive role current or foreseeable laws, enforcement mechanisms, or court proceedings might play in the struggle for animal liberation. For these activists, the government is not only historically rooted in and constitutionally committed to the ideology of speciesism but also daily subject to the influence of powerful special interests that perpetuate speciesist practices as a matter of law. These activists see the government as part of the problem, not part of the solution.

Violence versus Nonviolence

Despite his belief in the necessity of working with the government, Douglass was to his dying day a staunch supporter of "agitation," a commitment poignantly captured by Philip Foner's description of a meeting that took place some weeks before Douglass's death. "In the early days of 1895, a young Negro student living in New England journeyed to Providence, Rhode Island, to seek the advice of the aged Frederick Douglass who was visiting that city. As the interview drew to a close the youth said, 'Mr. Douglass, you have lived in both the old and new dispensations. What have you to say to a young Negro just starting out? What should he do?' The patriarch lifted his head and replied, 'Agitate! Agitate! Agitate!' (Foner 1950:371).

To our ears, Douglass's prescription might sound like a license to lawlessness, but this is not what he meant. For most of his life, Douglass, like the vast majority of abolitionists, favored only nonviolent forms of agitation: peaceful assemblies, rallies, the distribution of pamphlets and other materials depicting the plight of slaves, and petitions—measures that collectively were referred to as "moral suasion." People were to be persuaded that slavery was wrong and ought to be abolished through appeals to their reason, their sense of justice, and their human compassion, not coerced to agree through violence or intimidation.

On this point Garrison and Douglass, who disagreed about much, spoke with one voice. When Garrison said abolitionists were not to do evil that good may come, he meant that they were not to do evil *even to slaveholders, even in pursuit of emancipation*. As he saw it, respect for the higher moral law requires that all efforts made in the name of emancipation, whether immediatist or gradualist and whether in concert with the Union or apart from it, treat all persons respectfully and thus nonviolently.

Not all abolitionists agreed. David Walker (1830) was one; a free black from Virginia, Walker called for massive slave uprisings. "Kill or be killed," he cried out. His *Appeal*, first published in 1829, is said to have influenced Nat Turner as he planned his bloody insurrection in Southampton, Virginia. John Brown was another who did not agree. His legendary raid on Harpers Ferry divided the nation. Southern slave interests with one voice condemned his band of terrorists even as many abolitionists, including Henry David Thoreau, viewed the same acts as noble and inspiring. Brown, Thoreau observes, had the "peculiar doctrine that a man has a perfect right to interfere by force with the slave holder, in order to rescue the slave." And Thoreau's judgment? "I agree with him" (in Oates 1984:365). Although Captain Brown's raid was a military disaster, his call to arms was a portent of things to come, and his last words, written just before his execution, proved to be prophetic: "I, John Brown, am now convinced that the crimes of this guilty land cannot be purged except by blood" (in ibid.:351). In less than a year, the country was at war with itself.

On this matter, today's animal rightists, if not unanimously then at least solidly, align themselves with Garrison and Douglass. Evil, in the form of violence, should not be done to any human being, even in pursuit of animal liberation, and anyone who would perform such an act, whatever that person might say or believe, would not be acting according to the higher moral law that should guide and inform the animal rights movement.

This prohibition against violence to human and other forms of sentient life, however, does not necessarily carry over to property. Most of slavery's opponents understood this. If the cost of freeing a slave was damaged, destroyed, or in the case of slaves themselves, stolen property, then Garrison, Douglass, and most (but not all) of their abolitionist peers were prepared to accept such violence.

The same is true of many of today's animal rights advocates. Let me be perfectly honest. Some animal rightists obviously believe that violent acts against property carried out in the name of animal liberation, as well as the liberation of animals themselves (the theft of property, given current law), are perfectly justified. Other animal rightists disagree, believing that a principled commitment to the "higher moral law" of nonviolence must be maintained even in the treatment of property.

How many believe the one, how many believe the other, no one, I think, can say. What we can say, and what we should say, is this: it is just as false, just as misleading, and possibly just as dishonest to say that the animal rights movement is a nonviolent movement as it is to say that it is a terrorist movement. The movement to abolish slavery was neither just the one nor just the other. Of the movement to abolish animal exploitation, the same can and should be said. Those who do not say it, whatever their motivations, distort rather than describe the truth. Or so I believe.

Understanding Animal Rights Violence

But if we cannot know how many activists are prepared to use violence against property in the name of animal liberation, the preceding remarks may at least help us understand why they are prepared to do so. Their reasons, I suggest, are as follows.

To understand their motivation, it is not enough to say, "They are abolitionists," since some abolitionists abjure the use of violence not only against persons but also against property. Rather, those who are prepared to use violence are likely to be abolitionists who, first, cannot morally accept reformist means toward realizing their abolitionist ends (for example, they insist on replacement before, not after, reduction and refinement in the case of animals used in research) and, second, cannot rationally believe that the government, as presently or foreseeably constituted, can or will be of any real help in achieving the kind of revolutionary animal liberation they envision.

These activists, I conjecture, reject reformist measures because, like Garrison, they are not willing to accept "doing evil that good may come." Moreover, they have abandoned faith in the government, again like Garrison, because they see the government as being in collusion with and promoting the interests of those who perpetuate the evil they wish to see abolished: the evil of animal exploitation. Impatient with the pace and manner of change and convinced of the prejudice and injustice of the government, which by its laws makes animal exploitation possible, these activists have recourse to the only meaningful form of protest they believe is available to them: violent protest, in the form of damage to or destruction of property. Many there are who will view such behavior as immoral or imprudent. Whether it is the one or the other, my more modest point is that it is intelligible, predictable even, and that those who wish to understand animal rights violence do well first to understand the convictions that fueled the activism of Garrison, Douglass, John Brown, and their followers.

How to Lessen Animal Rights Violence

This violence is something that everyone, both friend and foe of animal rights, must lament, something we all wish could be prevented. The question is how to do so. How might we prevent if not all then at least many of the acts we all wish would not occur?

Here we arrive at a question that should give all people of goodwill pause. It is this question, I think, rather than questions about the moral or legal justification of violence, to which we might more profitably give our time, attention, imagination, and labor.

My own (very) modest proposal is this. Although Garrison-like abolitionists cannot support reformist measures, they can support *incremental abolitionist change*, change that involves stopping the utilization of nonhuman animals for one purpose or another. One goal, for example, might be not fewer animals used in cosmetic or industrial testing but no animals used for this purpose. Other goals might be not fewer dogs "sacrificed" in dog labs, or fewer primates "studied" in maternal deprivation research, or fewer goats shot and killed in weapons testing, but no animals used in each of these (and an indefinite number of other possible) cases.

A shared agenda of this type could set forth objectives that animal rights abolitionists, scientific policy makers, and biomedical researchers, for example, could agree on and work collaboratively to achieve; as such, it would go a long way toward reducing animal rights violence. It would demonstrate that it is possible to achieve incremental abolitionist goals by acting nonviolently within the system. This in turn would help defuse the idea that such goals can be achieved only by acting violently outside the system.

I neither say nor believe that such bold steps would eliminate all animal rights violence. What I do believe is that they would help lessen the amount of violence. I also believe that unless we find imaginative, good-faith ways of trying to prevent animal rights violence instead of simply devising more (and more severe) ways of punishing its perpetrators (which is the way defenders of slavery attempted to deal with those who used violence in the name of slave liberation), unless we practice preventive ethics in this quarter, animal rights violence will increase in the coming months and years. Indeed, as things stand at present, the wonder of it is not that there is animal rights violence but that there is not more of it.

Works Cited

Channing, William Ellery. 1835. "Essay on Slavery." In *The Works of William E. Channing*, 6 vols., 2:123–33. Boston: Anti-Slavery Office.

Douglass, Frederick. 1845. *Narrative of the Life of Frederick Douglass, an American Slave. Written by Himself.* Boston: Anti-Slavery Office.

Foner, Philip S. 1950. *Frederick Douglass: A Biography.* New York: Citadel.

Francione, Gary, and Tom Regan. 1992. "A Movement's Means Create Its Ends." *The Animals' Agenda*, January/February, pp. 40–43.

Garrison, William Lloyd. 1831. "Immediate Emancipation." *The Liberator*, September 3, pp. 1–2.

Oates, Stephen B. 1984. *To Purge This Land with Blood: A Biography of John Brown.* Amherst: University of Massachusetts Press.

Walker, David, 1830. *Walker's Appeal, in Four Articles; together with a Preamble, to the Colored Citizens of the World, and Very Expressly, to Those of the United States of America.* Boston: David Walker.

8

IVORY TOWERS SHOULD NOT A PRISON MAKE

"Ivory Towers Should Not a Prison Make" was first present-
ed at the 1991 Eastern Division meetings of the American Philosophical Association as part of a symposium on philosophy and advocacy jointly sponsored by the American Society for Value Inquiry and the International Society
for Environmental Ethics. Although originally written for an audience of
academic moral philosophers, the paper raises issues that should be of interest to a general readership.

That a symposium on philosophy and advocacy was held at all suggests
how much moral philosophy has changed in the past fifty years. During this
time moral philosophers have become increasingly involved in a variety of
subdisciplines, including health-care ethics, business ethics, legal ethics,
research ethics, veterinary ethics, and environmental ethics. Today's commonplace is yesterday's heresy. The very suggestion that a moral philosopher would have anything to do with ethical issues that arise in the world of
business or in the practice of veterinary medicine would have provoked
sneers or laughter from the vast majority of moral philosophers only two
generations removed.

Although the growth of applied ethics (as this development is sometimes
called) has been for the most part positive, some moral philosophers have
encountered more than a little hostility, especially when their ideas call for
radical changes and the philosophers join in agitating for their implementation. As with other philosophers who are advocates, this certainly has been
true in my case, both on the campus where I teach, North Carolina State
University, and at other universities. I document some aspects of this hostility in the following pages. Because nothing good is likely to come from
identifying the persons who attacked me, I judge it best that my accusers go
unnamed. Moreover, I would be remiss if I failed to note here, as I write these

introductory words almost a decade after this chapter's composition, that my experience during the intervening years has changed for the better. The responses of faculty and staff, including those whose values and careers are most directly affected as animal rights attracts increasing public support, have lately been far more respectful than the treatment I met with during the period when this chapter was written. My hope is that the future will be more like the present than the past.

While philosophers who advocate a cause need to be thick-skinned, the hostility and rancor they encounter can quickly shade into attacks on moral philosophy in general, something I illustrate in the pages to follow. In becoming advocates for the ideas about which they theorize, moral philosophers do more than risk their own good names and peace of mind; they also put the reputation of their profession at risk.

Are these weighty enough reasons for moral philosophers to be content with trying to understand the world, leaving to others the task of changing it? I argue not. Moral philosophers, like other concerned citizens, should be willing to take the strength of their convictions out of their studies and into the streets. Although it is quieter and more comfortable inside, our ivory towers should not a prison make.

Originally published as "The Business of the Ethical Philosopher," in *Explorations of Value*, ed. Thomas Magnell, 93–104 (Amsterdam and Atlanta: Rodopi). Reprinted with permission of the publisher.

In the opening pages of *Principia Ethica*, the young G. E. Moore (for Moore was not yet thirty when he wrote this historically influential work) remarks that "it is not the business of the ethical philosopher to give personal advice or exhortation" (1903:3). Moore is not saying that ethical philosophers overstep the bounds of their discipline if they endorse some general rule or principle or declare that certain traits of character are virtuous. In *Principia* Moore himself does both. Rather, he is arguing that in their professional capacity, ethical philosophers ought not issue advice or exhortation regarding facts that are, in his words, "unique, individual, absolutely particular" (ibid.). "There are," Moore writes, "far too many persons, things and events in the world, past, present, or to come, for a discussion of their individual merits to be embraced by any science. Ethics, therefore," he goes on to say, "does not deal at all with facts of this nature, facts that are unique, individual, absolutely particular; facts with which such studies as history, geography, astronomy, are compelled, at least in part, to deal." He thus concludes, in the words already quoted, that ethical philosophers should not render judgments on such matters.

I think Moore is partly right, and—maybe—partly wrong. He is right certainly when he implies that no ethical philosophy can possibly address all the "facts" of the sort he describes, of which, as he notes, there are "many million" (1903:3). He is mistaken, however, to the extent that he implies that ethical philosophers necessarily have wandered off the straight and narrow path of their profession if they choose to consider *some* such facts—for example, the particular cases of Baby Jane Doe, the executions of Sacco and Vanzetti, or the construction of the Tellico Dam. To my mind, it is entirely appropriate for moral philosophers to consider the "individual merits" of such matters and, depending on their findings, to register their judgment for or against.

Possibly Moore would agree. I say possibly because, in evaluating the merits of the Baby Jane Doe case, for example, we are not evaluating just one "unique, individual, absolutely particular" fact. In the nature of the case, we are obliged to consider a constellation of many such facts (for example, the child's present condition and the evidence for alternative predictions about her future), not simply one fact standing alone, in isolation from everything else. Thus, if Moore means that ethical philosophers should not assess the merits of such constellations of facts, I believe he is mistaken, whereas if he believes that it is only "atomic facts," as it were, that are beyond our reach, then perhaps he is correct.

There are, of course, other things that ethical philosophers will need if they decide to take their professional training out of their studies and test the turbulent waters of real-life controversies. In addition to having the relevant facts (and the more, the better), one also needs to think about these facts and related matters with logical care. One needs, too, a good dose of conceptual clarity, a nose for logical nuance, and a mind cleansed (as far as this is possible) of insupportable bias or prejudice. In addition, one needs some well-considered moral principles about the nature of the right and the just, good and evil—a tall order, by any reckoning, and an ideal that we perhaps will never fully realize, try as we might.

For many moral philosophers alive today, what I am saying is more in the nature of orthodoxy than heresy. Applied, or practical, ethics is part of the contemporary moral philosopher's bag of tools, and all that I am saying is that it is appropriate that we have and use these tools responsibly in the conduct of our professional lives. That this conception of ethical philosophy represents an important change from the conception dominant as recently as fifty years ago will be evident to anyone familiar with twentieth-century Anglo-American ethics. The sorts of questions ("metaethical" questions, as they were called) that set the agenda for ethical philosophers back then—questions about the meaning of the language of morals and the nature of moral disagreement—have been not answered but rather tabled, at least temporarily. The cyclical swing of thought being what it is, I have no doubt that we are in store for another heavy, healthy dose of metaethical philosophy in the coming years. But for now at least, finding a place for applied ethics within the profession is mainstream—"to the max," one might say.

Advocacy

Still, there is a difference (or so I am willing to concede) between applied ethics and the topic I intend to explore: advocacy and values. In one sense, it is true, anyone who argues for any conclusion, moral or otherwise, can be said to advocate that conclusion. Suppose we call this the logical sense of advocacy. In this sense, Immanuel Kant advocated the categorical imperative; Moore, some form of utilitarianism; and Bertrand Russell—well, Russell advocated almost everything, at one time or another. A second sense of advocacy involves something more, the "something more" that emerges from standard dictionary definitions of the nouns *advocate* and *advocacy* and the verb *to advocate*. Thus the noun *advocate* is defined as "a person who defends, vindicates, or espouses a cause by argument"; the noun *advocacy*, as "an act of pleading for or giving verbal support to a cause"; and the verb *to advocate*, as "to plead in favor of; support or urge by argument; recommend publicly" (*Random House College Dictionary*, rev. ed., s.vv. "advocate," "advocacy"). What unifies these definitions is the idea of doing something in favor of—defending, vindicating, supporting, pleading for—a cause. Suppose we refer to this sense of advocacy as the normative sense (about which more in a moment). In arguing for their respective philosophical views about the indefinability of good and the baldness of the present king of France, neither Moore nor Russell is an advocate in this sense, for in making the respective claims each did, neither saw himself to be arguing, let alone pleading, for a cause.

This concept of advocacy—the one that is bound up with advocating in favor of a cause, the one I have called the normative sense—differs from the logical sense. Philosophically considered, a work of advocacy in the normative sense is one that, while attempting to adhere to standards appropriate to the profession, articulates certain goals (the cause that the work itself advocates). These goals may find their original articulation in such a work, or they may predate the work. For example, works of advocacy by environmental philosophers, feminist philosophers, socialist or capitalist philosophers, and animal liberation or animal rights philosophers may be of either kind; they may constitute the original articulation of the relevant goals, or they may add their voice to preexisting goals. These goals, in turn, may be (to create a new word) status-quoist, reformist, or abolitionist. That is, the cause advocated may be (1) to retain the current state of affairs (to retain certain policies or practices in particular), (2) to reform the current state of affairs (to keep certain policies or practices in general while reforming them in particular ways), or (3) to abolish—to bring to an end—certain policies or practices. The history of philosophy is crowded with works of advocacy in this (the normative) sense, works that fit one or another of these descriptions.

In addition to the logical and normative senses of advocacy, which to my mind are beyond philosophical suspicion or controversy, there is a third sense that needs to be distinguished. We could call this the *political* sense. In this sense, advocacy involves more than affirming a position (the logical sense) and more than writing an essay or book that advocates a cause (the normative sense). The political sense involves *active public participation in efforts to forward the cause*, efforts that go beyond advocacy in the logical or normative senses to include such modes of advocacy as attempting to exert pressure on those who hold political office; helping to organize boycotts; speaking at conferences, rallies, or demonstrations with the intention of informing or empowering other activists; or participating in marches, sit-ins, and other forms of civil disobedience, all in the name of furthering "the cause." The question now to be asked is whether this kind of advocacy of a cause—what I have called *political* advocacy—is "the business of the ethical philosopher."

My own answer to this question is no. In saying this, I do not mean that philosophers should not actively engage in such political means of advocacy as rallies, demonstrations, and civil disobedience. On the contrary, not only do I believe that such political advocacy is entirely appropriate; I have myself been a political advocate in both antiwar and the animal rights movements.

What I mean in answering the question as I do is this: when philosophers engage in such activities as these, they do so *as concerned citizens, not as ethical philosophers*. Of course, the grounds for their political advocacy (their reasons for believing the cause is just or right) are likely to be distinctively philosophical—the very grounds they may have articulated in the essays or books that advocate the cause in the normative sense. My point is only that, once philosophers enter the political arena—the arena of political pressure and public protest—they do so not as philosophers who happen to be citizens but as citizens who happen to be philosophers. So, in my view, it is not the business of the ethical philosopher, *qua* ethical philosopher, to be an advocate in the political sense. Philosophers who engage in such extraphilosophical activities do so not in the name of philosophy but in the name of political or social change. Which is fine, I hasten to add; it is just not philosophy. I return to this matter later.

But it *is* philosophy, I also hasten to add, when, as often happens, philosophical advocates of a cause offer a summary of their philosophical advocacy—their normative position. Suppose the philosophical advocate is invited to a campus or some other public venue to give a forty-five-minute talk for the general public. Is it reasonable to assume that the finer details, the nuances, of, say, a 400-page book can be condensed into forty-five minutes? Only the authors of *Cliffs Notes* will be tempted to suppose so. Nevertheless, it is not unreasonable to expect and demand *something* by way of philosophy—to expect and demand that the ethical philosopher provide something (a sketch, in such a case) by way of philosophical advocacy in the normative sense. Granted, it is damnably difficult to say in a comparatively few words what required many more words to say to one's own best satisfaction. Still, even within these time constraints, and even in the face of an audience of the philosophically unwashed, ethical philosophers *can do* ethical philosophy—that is, they can allude to (at least some of) the relevant facts, exhibit the logical form of (at least some of) the most important arguments, diagnose (at least some of) the possible prejudices, and so on. It is not philosophy at its best and fullest, but this is no reason to say that it is not or cannot be philosophy at all.

Because more and more ethical philosophers are turning their attention to advocacy in the normative sense, they are increasingly finding themselves in the position I have just described. Philosophers working in health-care ethics, business ethics, and research ethics, for example, regularly participate in conferences where the majority of those attending are not professional philosophers. I believe that this is a salutary development, both for the profession and for society at large, but it is a mixed blessing. The very increase in philosophers' participation in society's attempts to address the major moral issues of the day can create a family of unwelcome problems, some personal, some of more general interest to the profession. As ethical philosophers, I believe we are well advised to be aware of some of these problems. At least my experience, in response to my advocacy, suggests as much.

That experience has been largely gained from my involvement in the animal rights movement. A number of my philosophical writings advocate animal rights in both the logical and the normative senses (Regan 1983, 1985). The same is true of many of my public lectures, including those presented on various campuses. Moreover, as I have already indicated, I have also been an advocate of animal rights in the political sense (at sit-ins, protests, rallies, and the like). Philosophically, the position I advocate is abolitionist. It argues that the nonhuman animals who are, for example, raised for food, killed for reasons of fashion, and "sacrificed" in the name of science are treated unjustly; that the injustice of these practices cannot be eliminated by reforming them in various ways (for example, by increasing the size of cages); and that, therefore, the right thing to do is to abolish these practices altogether.

Whether true or not (and the truth of the animal rights position is not at issue here), this position certainly can be perceived as a threat to the interests of others—those whose careers and livelihoods are tied to business as usual in commercial animal agriculture, the fur industry, and the biomedical industrial complex, to name three of many examples. As I have discovered, some of those who are threatened, including high-ranking academicians, voice their disfavor with my ideas about animal rights in the vocabulary of slander.

In what follows I relate some of my experiences. In doing so, I hope I will not be misunderstood. I have not chosen to share these slices of my life with a view to soliciting sympathy for my undeserved victimization. My interests, rather, are to determine what, if anything, might be learned from the treatment I have received as an advocate of a cause; to consider how this might possibly benefit other academic philosophers who are contemplating becoming or who already are advocates, in both the normative and political senses; and, generalizing on my experience, to speculate about some of the threats and challenges we face not individually and alone but collectively, as a profession.

Attack the Philosopher

As my experience illustrates, philosophical advocates of a cause may need to be prepared to encounter vicious personal and demeaning professional attacks. By way of example (and virtually all that follows has been written about me and is in the public domain), I have been called a dangerous zealot, a firebrand, and a rabble-rousing demagogue. I have been likened to Hermann Göring and to monomaniacal mental patients who think they are Jesus Christ or Napoléon; on one occasion, I was described as the Jim Jones of the animal rights movement. Referring to my campus lectures, opponents have accused me of advocating violence; of spreading lies; of being antiscience, antirational, and anti-intellectual; of asserting that I have the right to impose by violent means my notion of ethics on others; and of inflaming my audiences to commit unlawful acts. All these charges are false. On another occasion there was the suggestion that I am the "point man," so to speak, for laboratory break-ins, and on still another it was implied that I may have been involved in the crime of murder. Again, both claims are false. Finally, my book *The Case for Animal Rights* (Regan 1983) has been dismissed as entirely lacking in scholarly merit, a lengthy, tendentious non sequitur in which I substitute zealotry for reasoned argument—a work in which my appeals are entirely emotional.

Now no one can relish being the target of ad hominem attacks, of remarks that slander one's character or degrade one's professional standing. All this is bad enough. What is worse—and here I believe my experience does not differ qualitatively from that of many other philosophers who advocate other causes—is the realization that the attacks aimed at me are part of a larger national strategy involving powerful political figures and professional organizations. By way of example, consider first the following statement contained in the American Medical Association's "Animal Research Action Plan": "The animal activist movement must be shown to be not only antiscience but also . . . responsible for violent and illegal acts that endanger life and property" (American Medical Association 1989:2).

Next consider these remarks by Frederick K. Goodwin, M.D., the former administrator of the Alcohol, Drug Abuse, and Mental Health Association. "The animal rights movement is, in large part, a young persons' movement, and it is made up of young people who tend to substitute sentiment for reason. In effect, they are saying, 'Because I *feel* strongly about not using animals in research, it's true for me.'" Goodwin goes on to dismiss, in a tone of righteous indignation, what he calls the "facile, pathetically misinformed, and/or dishonest arguments" animal rights advocates urge against animal research (1993:6).

Finally, consider the declamations that the former U.S. representative Vin Weber (R-Minn.), founder of the Animal Welfare Caucus, made in an invitation to a fundraising event featuring the former Health and Human Services secretary Dr. Louis Sullivan: "It is my pleasure to invite you to meet a national leader in the fight to counteract the mindless emotionalism and violent tactics of the animal rights movement" (Weber 1990:1). Later in his invitation, Congressman Weber declares that "the tactics employed by the animal rights movement are nothing short of terrorism. . . . Calling animal rights activists' destructive methods arguments is giving them too much credit" (2).

The list goes on. Certainly there is no difficulty in multiplying examples of this rhetoric of derision as practiced by people in high places—and as my earlier remarks confirm, in lower places, too. As the examples cited show, the comments that some research scientists have made about Tom Regan in particular had already been made by their national leaders about the animal rights movement in general. As I have said, this is important to understand, for the more an ethical philosopher's advocacy threatens powerful political and economic forces with a vested interest in the status quo, the greater the risk that the philosopher will encounter and be called on to endure the slanderous attacks of those who are threatened. Individual ethical philosophers who choose to run this risk normally stand alone, without much by way of organized interest in or support from the larger philosophical community. Perhaps this is as it should be. After all, philosophers who align themselves with a cause choose to do so; arguably they must be prepared to reap the sometimes bitter fruits of their advocacy. Nevertheless, the attack on advocates, if my experience is any guide, can cross the boundaries of the personal and encroach on the profession, so that the two—attacks on the individual and attacks on the profession—can become all but inseparable. The following two examples illustrate this point.

Attack the Discipline

The first example involves a scientist who registered his displeasure with my having been invited to his campus. He noted that I lack "an adequate scientific background" (which is fair enough, as far as it goes). He then argued, however, that for this reason my presentation would be not "open and objective, but a sophisticated rationalization of an emotionally [sic] and biased point of view." This is a familiar theme, at least as familiar as C. P. Snow's seminal work on differences between the scientific culture and the humanities (Snow 1959). Viewed from the perspective of the scientific component of Snow's two cultures, either one reasons from "an adequate scientific background," in which case one is able to conduct an "open and objective" discussion, or one speaks without the benefit of "an adequate scientific background," in which case one can at best muster something by way of "a sophisticated rationalization" of an emotional and biased point of view. Given this perspective, to the extent that ethical philosophers lack a strong scientific background or are perceived to lack one, they will be seen as lacking the ability to offer an open and objective presentation and will instead be seen as quasi (or pseudo-?) professionals who are able only to evince their emotions behind the smoke and mirrors of intellectual sophistry. In this way, individual ethical philosophers who advocate a cause in the normative sense, and most especially those who also engage in political advocacy, can trigger slumbering dogmas about the nature of ethical philosophy. In a very real sense, part of the attempt to discredit the individual practitioner of ethical philosophy can consist in attempts to discredit the practice.

A second variation on this main theme was made clear to me by the comments of an influential psychology professor who happened to be among the most vicious in his personal attacks on me. Along with making these attacks, this professor commented on what he saw as the arrogance of ethical philosophers who, because they "study ethics," assume that they are "the guardians of other people's ethics." "In this country," this particular professor continues, "personal ethics is a matter for the individual conscience, and neither priest nor philosopher have an inherent right, or a widely acknowledged special expertise, that allows them to dictate to others, certainly not by violent means, the ethical judgments they should make."

These comments are perfectly general; they are aimed not at me in particular but at ethical philosophers in general. Even if we ignore the reference to "violent means," these comments, in my view, are confused. I do not know a single ethical philosopher who views him- or herself as "the guardian of other people's ethics," or who believes that he or she is in a position to "dictate" what ethical judgments others should make. Of course, ethical philosophers often advocate controversial ethical positions. In doing so, moreover, they often argue in favor of, defend, attempt to vindicate, or support a cause that is at odds with the ethical judgments of others. Nonetheless, neither of these truths entails anything about the philosophical advocate's assuming "guardianship" of other people's ethics or "dictating" to others what ethical judgments they should make. How widespread these misunderstandings are, I do not know. My own experience, however, both on my campus and beyond, suggests that they are very widespread indeed. Once again, therefore, the advocacy of individual ethical philosophers can occasion vigorous if misinformed indictments of ethical philosophy in general. Once again, therefore, part of the attempt to discredit the individual practitioners of normative advocacy can consist in attempts to discredit the practice.

Perhaps we might learn something useful from the family portrait of ethical philosophers that emerges from the preceding. To begin with, it appears that the nonphilosophical community of scholars has not kept abreast of changes in philosophy. Although it is true, as I observed earlier, that the metaethical questions that dominated Anglo-American moral philosophy for a large part of the twentieth century have been shelved rather than answered, it seems very unlikely that, when we return to them, we will do so only to exhume the corpse of logical positivism, which seems to be the epistemological ideology that underlies the unflattering family portrait of ethical philosophers informing the previously cited complaints—the disreputable image of what it is to *be* an ethical philosopher.

Relatedly, the sheer staying power of the assumption that science is "objective" whereas arguments about value are "emotional" attests to the not-too-blissful ignorance from which some academic scientists suffer regarding much of the recent work in the philosophy of science. Recognizing this fact might helpfully remind us of the importance of familiarizing the next generation of scientists with this literature, lest this harmful assumption continue to hold sway. There is thus a real need for philosophers, both ethical philosophers and philosophers of science, to make greater contributions to the education of scientists in our classrooms and beyond. But doing this will probably not be an easy task. If ethics is denigrated because it is *subjective and emotional* (unlike science, which is valorized because it is *objective and rational*), and if ethical philosophers are perceived to be people who want to *dictate* other people's values (unlike scientists, who *discover* the truth), then the sometimes cool, sometimes hostile reception many academic scientists shower on the suggestion that their students need a course in ethics is hardly remarkable. Clearly, the challenge that ethical philosophers must face in discussions about curricular change in the sciences is likely to be both formidable and protracted.

However these matters are to be resolved—and I claim no special wisdom regarding the solutions—my central points are these: that philosophical advocates of a cause, while they speak for themselves, often are perceived as representatives of ethical philosophy in general; that when, as sometimes happens, efforts are made to discredit the individual philosopher, these efforts sometimes will include attempts to discredit the profession; and that in choosing to assume the role of advocate of a cause, individual ethical philosophers should realize that, like it or not, they may be called on not only to defend their views and endure slanderous attacks on their person but also to explain and defend the discipline of ethical philosophy. None of this, in my view, constitutes a sufficient reason for philosophers to avoid the role of advocate, in the normative *or* political sense, about which I say more later, but it does go some way toward suggesting the variety and magnitude of the challenges one might face if one does decide to become an advocate.

Academic Freedom

I turn now to my final point, which concerns academic freedom. Those who have most vehemently attacked me, both personally and as a scholar, have frequently insisted that they were not denying my right to free speech. (As one of my principal detractors wrote: "Anyone, from Farrakhan to Regan, has a right to speak on a university campus no matter how abhorrent his views are to any segment of the community.") This sounds eminently fair, and it would be fair if philosophical advocates, including those with "abhorrent views," could be assured that the traditions of academic freedom will prevail in their case. Not surprisingly, such a guarantee requires sustained (if not quite eternal) vigilance. .

On my own campus, for example, certain individuals who strongly disagree with my views on animal rights once objected to my participation in a campus program because (and here I quote) "North Carolina State University should not be perceived as supporting Tom Regan's position on animal rights because it might offend research funding organizations and cause the loss of grants." In this case, fortunately, the sponsors refused to be intimidated, and the program went on as scheduled. It was only by accident, however, that I discovered the existence of this attempt to silence my voice— and this on my own campus, where I had then been teaching for twenty-five years.

On other campuses the main storyline differs. Sometimes objections are voiced because (roughly speaking) I am said to be a violent terrorist who will incite my audience to riot (which is why, in some cases, uniformed police and other law-enforcement officers have attended my campus lectures); at other times they are voiced because (and here I quote from a letter by one of my detractors) "the issue is not one of intellectual debate consecrated by our commitment to academic freedom, but rather one of *anti-intellectual actions* that have been specifically condemned by our Academic Senate" (emphasis in original). Whether one who practices "anti-intellectual actions" should be permitted the academic freedom to perform them is less than clear.

Nevertheless, despite efforts to the contrary, my freedom to speak has to the best of my knowledge never been denied, either at my own campus or elsewhere. In this I have been fortunate indeed. Clearly, if those people who had invited me to speak had failed to insist on my right to do so, I would have been denied the exercise of this fundamental right.

This, then, is another dimension of advocacy that is worth considering. Precisely because the cause advocated can threaten powerful special interests, one can anticipate various efforts aimed at silencing the advocate. Moreover, when the advocate is an ethical philosopher, and in view of the fact that attempts to discredit the advocate sometimes include allegations that discredit ethical philosophy, those of us who are ethical philosophers have, if anything, an even greater obligation to ensure that the traditions of academic freedom prevail.

Perhaps all that we should do as professionals can be done effectively by using the resources of already existing committees within, say, the American Association of University Professors and the American Philosophical Association. If this is true, then by all means let us honor Occam's sage advice and not multiply committees beyond necessity. But it is worth asking ourselves, both those of us who, in our philosophical work, advocate changes in the status quo and those who do not, whether something more is needed, even if we conclude, after informed reflection, that nothing is. On this matter even Moore, who had well considered views about the business of the ethical philosopher, would agree.

Lastly, I return to the matter of political advocacy—taking part in rallies, protests, demonstrations, civil disobedience, and other public campaigns carried out in the hope of changing the status quo. As moral philosophers, should we be willing to participate in such activities, or should we studiously avoid them?

My own position, as indicated earlier, is that we should be willing to take the strength of our convictions out of our studies and into the streets. It is, I think, entirely appropriate for moral philosophers to agitate politically and publicly for a cause in which they believe. Indeed, I am inclined to go further. By my lights, a willingness to gather with other partisans at the barricades, so to speak, is part of our wholeness as moral agents in the world; it is *a* way (though not the only one) to assess our moral integrity, a topic to which I return in the following chapter. It is a strange understanding of moral development, I think, that says we have gone as far as we should when we have sought merely to understand the world, there being no need to join with others in trying to change it.

Nevertheless, it is not in our role as moral philosophers that we are called on to take this further step; rather, doing so is part of the larger human quest for integrity and wholeness. Our training in and commitment to the highest standards of academic moral philosophy do not easily prepare us to take this further step; in fact, they may discourage it. But our fascination with ideas, as important, exhilarating, and time-consuming as this can be, offers no excuse for refusing to act in pursuit of what we profess to believe. In this respect, no one holds us hostage but ourselves. And our ivory towers should not a prison make.

Works Cited

American Medical Association. 1989. *AMA Animal Research Action Plan.* Washington, D.C.: American Medical Association.

Goodwin, Frederick K. 1993. "In Animal Rights Debate, the Only Valid Moderates Are Researchers." *The Scientist* 67 (Sept.): 6.

Moore, George Edward. 1903. *Principia Ethica.* Cambridge: Cambridge University Press.

Regan, Tom. 1983. *The Case for Animal Rights.* Berkeley: University of California Press.

———. 1985. "The Case for Animal Rights." In *In Defense of Animals,* ed. Peter Singer, 13–26. Oxford: Blackwell.

Snow, C. P. 1959. *The Two Cultures and the Scientific Revolution.* Cambridge: Cambridge University Press.

Weber, Vin. 1990. Letter of invitation. House of Representatives, Washington, D.C., September.

9

WORK, HYPOCRISY, AND INTEGRITY

In April 1997 I was honored to receive an invitation to make a plenary presentation at an international conference on business ethics held in Beijing under the auspices of the Chinese Academy of Sciences. Most of the conference presenters grappled with large themes, such matters as justice in the distribution of capital and the compatibility of the free market with traditional Chinese values, particularly Confucian ones.

In contrast, my paper deals with problems individuals face in their day-to-day life as employees, as workers, whether they work mowing lawns or sowing ideas. Many of us who earn a paycheck in the employ of someone else are troubled by some of the things our employers do; in fact, for some of us, some of what passes as "business as usual" goes against the grain of our consciences. For example, I work at a large university that routinely prepares students for careers in commercial animal agriculture and animal research. I view these ways of treating other-than-human animals as morally wrong. Yet here I am, still employed by North Carolina State University, still receiving my monthly pay, after more than thirty years on the faculty.

How is it possible for me or anyone in relevantly similar circumstances to reconcile what appears to be an irreconcilable contradiction? If people really believe that an employer is doing something immoral, should not their integrity force them to resign? If they do not resign, is that not tantamount to confessing that they really do not have the values they say they do? In a word, by staying on the job, have they not either compromised their moral integrity or demonstrated their moral hypocrisy?

This chapter presents my tentative answers to these questions. The pacifist physics professor who works in a department where other faculty are doing weapons research operates as my proxy. His pacifist ideals are comparable to my commitment to animal rights; the former are as important to him and his life as the latter are to me and mine. If I can credibly explain how he can continue in his employment and neither manifest hypocrisy nor lack integrity, then the same kind of explanation will be credible for others, myself included, who find themselves in relevantly similar circumstances. I argue that conformity with something I call a person's all-things-considered values is the proper basis for assessing an employee's hypocrisy and integrity and that this makes it possible (but never easy) for people to avoid being hypocrites and retain their integrity even when their employers are engaged in practices they judge to be immoral.

"Work, Hypocrisy, and Integrity" has not been previously published.

Like many other academicians, I am not part of the world of business in the ordinary sense of that term—not a banker, a manufacturer, or a stockbroker, for example. Nonetheless, like other people who earn a day's pay for a day's work, I am involved in the world of economic exchange as a worker, an employee. What I want to explore are problems that I assume are common for any worker, any employee, whatever that person's position in the company or institution for which that person works and wherever the place of employment, be it China or the United States. When it comes to ethical problems in the workplace, we all face similar dilemmas and occupy common, often perplexing moral ground.

I approach our shared ethical concerns from the perspectives I bring with me. I am a philosopher steeped in the traditions of Western thought generally and the tradition of twentieth-century Anglo-American analytic philosophy in particular. No doubt these perspectives may prove to be limitations, but I would slight other traditions and flatter my intelligence if I were to attempt to speak from perspectives other than my own.

The Problems

Many of us face a particular sort of conflict in our working lives. It is not that we dislike what we do, believe we are underpaid or undervalued, or cannot get along with our fellow workers or those above us, although these sorts of conflicts are common enough, at least in America. It is not even that we find our jobs unimportant or unrewarding, although many workers (again, at least in America) struggle internally because they do. The sort of conflict I have in mind is different.

What I have in mind is this: many employees think the company or institution that employs them is doing something wrong, something unethical. Nevertheless, they remain on the job. The conflict comes into view when we ask how we can make moral sense of this behavior. If workers really believe that an employer is doing something wrong, are they not sacrificing their moral integrity by collecting a paycheck? Alternatively, if they stay on the job and continue to profit from what they say they believe is wrong, are we not obliged to question whether they really have those values they say they do—the ones that lead them to judge that the employer is doing something wrong, something unethical? Are they not being hypocritical if, however much they say their values differ from their employer's, they nevertheless remain employed?

It is this sort of conflict, the one that concerns the ideas of integrity and hypocrisy, that I want to discuss.

Some Preliminaries

A number of preliminaries need to be explained. Notice, first, that the issue does not concern what really is right or wrong, about which systematic moral philosophers in the West differ as much as ordinary people everywhere. For example, some philosophers and many other people in America believe that the right thing to do is to follow the commands of God, whereas other Americans deny that there is a God to command anything and instead believe that we should do what will advance the good of society. Here we have a conflict in moral beliefs, and a good deal of moral philosophy, at least in the West, concerns itself with the question, "Which if either of these opposing positions is correct?"

As important as this sort of disagreement is, it is not the type of conflict I want to explore. The sort of conflict that concerns me involves what people (in this case, workers) *believe* is right and wrong, not the truth of such beliefs. In fact, the truth of their beliefs turns out to be totally irrelevant. An example should make this clearer.

Cigarette advertising is a divisive issue in America. Many Americans believe that the free market in cigarette advertising oversteps its moral boundaries when children are targeted as prospective customers. Defenders of placing cigarette ads near schools maintain that since the ads never target children, there is nothing wrong in placing the ads there. Each side believes its position to be true, and much ink has been spilled by partisans on both sides attempting to prove their point.

Although the conflict I wish to explore can arise within the cigarette advertising context, it has nothing to do with the truth of these two opposing positions. The conflict arises in a different way. For example, suppose an American woman is employed by one of her country's major cigarette manufacturers. Suppose she professes to believe that cigarette smoking is harmful, that her company targets ads at children by placing them near schools, and that it is wrong to market harmful products to children. This much granted, this woman faces the sort of conflict under review. That is, she represents herself as thinking that the company that employs her is doing something wrong, yet she continues to show up for work. If this worker has any moral integrity, how can she continue to behave as she does? Alternatively, if she continues to behave as she does (shows up for work and accepts her pay), questions arise about the sincerity of her professed beliefs. If she profits from something she professes to believe is wrong, are we not right to question whether she is being hypocritical in declaring what she believes?

Notice that these questions press themselves on us whether or not it is wrong to market harmful products to children. Put another way, the questions concern the moral character of the person who professes to have certain moral beliefs, not the truth of what that person professes to believe.

One thing seems clear—and here the predilections of my Western analytic philosophical baggage will be apparent. If we are to make headway in this inquiry, we need to spend some time examining the two ideas that define the questions. So let me first consider the notion of hypocrisy, reserving comments about integrity until later.

Moral Hypocrisy

The English word *hypocrisy* has its origin in the Greek *hypokrisia*, meaning "play as a part." The etymology is preserved in the contemporary meaning. Hypocrites are people who play a part. They represent themselves as being better than they are. Although hypocrisy is a form of deception, not all forms of deception involve hypocrisy. If to extricate himself from an uncomfortable situation a employer promises to review a worker's complaint without the slightest intention of doing so, then the worker has no doubt been deceived. But whether the employer is a hypocrite is a question yet to arise, let alone to have been answered.

Suspicions of the deception that helps define hypocrisy characteristically arise in some of life's most important domains—among friends and family, for example. I will limit my remarks to hypocrisy in a moral context in general and in employment in particular.

Questions of moral hypocrisy arise when there is a conflict between what people say they believe is true or right or just, on the one hand, and how they actually behave, on the other. If a worker says you should always clean your tools at the end of the day, and if at the end of the day this worker always cleans his tools, there is no basis for (no suspicion of) hypocrisy. If another worker says the same thing but at the end of the day fails to clean his tools, then we are not wrong to wonder whether he sincerely believes in the value of having clean tools. Suspicions of hypocrisy characteristically arise when people act in ways that contradict (go against or are inconsistent with) their professed values.

Not all conflicts of this type represent hypocrisy, however. We all sometimes fail to live up to our professed standards. For example, although I value truth, I have lied on occasion. I have sometimes said that I had done something when I knew full well that I had not, and I have sometimes said that I had not done something when I knew full well that I had. I doubt that I am exceptional. Even if America's first president, George Washington, really did say, "I cannot tell a lie," when he confessed to having chopped down a cherry tree, he did not say that he never lied.

Does this mean that I am being hypocritical when I say that I value truth? I do not think so. What the conflict between my values and my behavior illustrates is my moral fallibility. For a variety of reasons (selfishness is one, and weakness of will is another), I sometimes fail to honor my values in my life. Sometimes my actions contradict values in which I really believe. Because this is true, the mere fact that people behave in ways that are at odds with their values is not sufficient to prove that they are hypocrites.

What happens when we fail to live up to our values? In particular, how do we feel when our acts are at odds with our ethical beliefs? Well, characteristically we experience more or less intense feelings of shame or guilt, the intensity of the feelings varying with the degree of the perceived offense. We do not feel good about ourselves when we fail to act as we think we should. These feelings—guilt, shame, regret, or remorse—are the ones we should have if we sincerely believe in those moral values we profess to believe yet occasionally fail to honor in our lives.

Contrast this with the situation of people who profess to have certain moral values yet are not the least bit troubled when they fail to honor them. They say they value truth, for example, but they experience no guilt or shame when they lie to sell a product they know to be defective or dangerous. Their only concern is whether their lie is efficacious—whether (in this example) they get away with lying and make the sale.

Of such people I think we may truly say that they are hypocrites. They do not sincerely believe in the values they profess. If they did, they would be morally troubled when they fail to live up to them. They would feel guilty or ashamed. If such feelings are strangers to them, or if they believe these feelings have no rightful place in their lives, then we are right to believe that they do not have the values they profess to have. When they say they have them, they are being hypocritical. Their profession of values is not sincere but deceptive. At least, this is one (though possibly not the only) form hypocrisy takes.

Notice that if this is true, then hypocrisy depends on more than just the match between action and verbal expression. It depends on emotions as well. Even though two people might do the same thing (for example, say that they value truth and also tell a lie), one could be hypocritical, and the other not. The hypocrite is the person who does this and (1) feels no remorse, guilt, or shame in having done so or (2) does not believe that he or she should feel these emotions. People who do experience such feelings in the face of their moral failings, or at least believe that they should have these feelings, are not hypocrites. They are exemplars of the morally fallible beings that humans are. They honestly believe in certain values; they just fail to exemplify them in their own lives.

Here is another way to express this same point. If I sincerely believe in certain values (the importance of speaking the truth, for example), then I believe that these values should be *universalized*. I believe everyone should be bound by the obligation to speak the truth, myself included. This much granted, I also believe (and must believe, if my beliefs are sincere) that anyone who fails to abide by these values will feel some degree of guilt or shame or at least will recognize that they should feel this way. Hypocrites are people who profess to believe in certain moral values but who fail the tests of universalizability: they do not believe that they are duty bound to tell the truth (although they think everyone should be truthful), or they think that, when they say what they know to be false, there is nothing untoward in *their* not feeling guilt or shame (although they imply that everyone should).

While I think what I have said to this point captures hypocrisy in its paradigmatic guise, it is possible that hypocrisy has, if not a thousand, at least many faces. Perhaps there are limits to human moral failings. Consider a manufacturer who professes to believe that it is wrong to hire young children and pay them meager wages. Nevertheless, he continues to exploit his young workers, even though he says it makes him feel terrible. Perhaps we reach a point where we are forced to say, "If he *really* believed what he says he believes, he would stop doing what he is doing." Perhaps we reach a point where the sincerity of his professed beliefs is no longer credible, a point where we say, "He is not being honest with himself. If he really believed what he says he believes, he would stop behaving the way he does. Whatever the reason, he is deceiving himself." I am uncertain what to say about cases like this one, but even if they represent hypocrisy of a certain type, it is not hypocrisy in its paradigmatic form.

Moral Hypocrisy and Work

If we limit ourselves to hypocrisy in its paradigmatic form, what may we say in response to the question about hypocrisy in employment? The following, I think. People who remain employed by a company or institution that they profess to believe is doing something unethical are not necessarily hypocrites. Everything depends on these people's beliefs and feelings about the situation in which they find themselves. If they declare that their employer is doing something wrong but are not troubled about continuing their employment, the analysis I have sketched would support charging them with hypocrisy. If the conditions of their employment cause them to feel more or less morally uncomfortable, more or less guilty or ashamed, then it is difficult to see how the charge of hypocrisy could be made to stick. It is not their intention to deceive anyone when they profess to have the values they say they do.

True, such a person perhaps might be lacking in courage or willpower, especially if the worker judges the employer's conduct to be a great evil. Of such a person we might say, "Why don't you have the courage of your convictions and quit?" Still, people who lack the courage of their convictions are just that: weak willed. And weak-willed workers who remain on the job in the sort of circumstances hypothesized here are not proven to be hypocrites because they do so.

Moral Integrity

As I indicated earlier, questions involving integrity also arise in the employment context. The logic of the questions differs here, however, because we must assume that the employee is not hypocritical. The moral beliefs *are* sincerely held, and the feelings of guilt or shame that accompany moral failing *are* genuine. For example, imagine a professor of physics who is a pacifist. He believes that war is always wrong, writes and lectures about its immo-

rality, joins in public demonstrations against it, and participates in acts of
civil disobedience as another means of expressing his opposition. As it happens, some faculty in his department are engaged in weapons-development
research. The physicist is genuinely troubled by the conditions of his employment. No hypocrite, he. But while he is not a hypocrite, what should
we say of his integrity? Has he not compromised it by continuing to work
in a department where, given his universe of values, others are doing something wrong?

Before we can answer this question, we need to ask what integrity involves. Fundamentally, it seems, people demonstrate their integrity by dis-
playing steady commitment to those values they sincerely accept. They
possess what Plato, in the *Republic*, called *dikaisyne*, usually translated as "harmony of soul." They have a rich sense of the ordering of their values and of
the way to resolve such conflicts as might arise among those values. Whereas
others might succumb to various temptations, people of integrity characteristically do not give in and do not pretend. Although not infallible by any
means, people of integrity arguably are distinguished from others because
of the constancy with which they live the values they say they have. Such
people are whole, not divided against themselves, when it comes to values
professed and values exemplified. What could be more admirable, more
desirable than this?

A good deal more, as it turns out. Despite the positive aura associated
with its attribution, integrity itself is a problematic virtue, if a virtue at all.
The worst sorts of people can be and regrettably sometimes are steadfast in
their commitment to the family of values they uphold. For example, people
who traffic in illegal drugs can exhibit integrity: they can be fully committed to being who they are and doing what they do. The same was true of
devoted Nazis and other moral monsters. Because the notion of integrity is
independent of the values steadfastly upheld, we do well to wonder how great
a moral virtue it is.

Of course, if some conceptual sleight-of-hand could limit people of integrity to upholding the "right" values—for example, commitments to truth,
justice, or family—we might avoid these difficulties. At least we might appear to do so. Appearances can be deceiving, however, and they would be
deceiving in this particular case if we failed to take full measure of integrity's open-ended quality. The plain fact is that evil people—indeed, the worst
of the worst—can have integrity.

If the preceding is correct, the problem posed by the pacifist physicist
should be clear. A person of integrity is one who characteristically displays

steadfast commitment to his or her values. If the physics professor is a man of integrity, then we should expect him to be steadfast in his commitment to pacifism. If he is steadfast in his commitment to pacifism, however, then (arguably) he should not be working for an employer that supports weapons-development research. Yet this is precisely what he is doing. Would we not be correct, then, to conclude that the professor is lacking in integrity?

Although this line of reasoning has an initial plausibility, closer examination should give us pause. To begin with, even though the professor has pacifist values, he surely has other values, too—for example, values associated with providing for his family and using his education to advance knowledge. Moreover, even in the case of his pacifist beliefs, things are not simple. A world without war is the ideal for which all pacifists must work, but how do we get there? If we imagine that the physics professor believes that the most important decision individual pacifists must make concerns where and how they can contribute most effectively to achieving pacifism's ideal, and if he believes that he is more effective working and speaking "from the inside" than he would be if he changed his employment status, then it would be a mistake to maintain that he has lost or violated his integrity by remaining on the faculty. Just the opposite: remaining on the faculty would be perfectly consistent with his values, all things considered, and thus with his moral integrity.

Before we can assess someone's integrity, then, we must do more than determine whether that person's behavior sometimes conflicts with his or her professed values. We must also determine that person's entire set of values and the way he or she ranks or prioritizes those values. Behavior that is at odds with some professed values is not sufficient to ground the judgment of a lack of integrity.

But behavior that is at odds with a person's all-things-considered values arguably is different. If the physics professor declares that his pacifist values are his most important values, and if he avows that it is wrong to do anything that is in any way associated with designing or developing weapons, including working where this is done, then (assuming he is not a hypocrite) we are right to question his integrity. People of integrity will not *live lives* that conflict with their all-things-considered values. Indeed, given the logic of the concept of integrity, people of integrity cannot do this.

Although this much seems clear, a question remains concerning whether people of integrity can occasionally fail to honor their all-things-considered values. Here I am asking not whether people of integrity can live lives that conflict with their values, all things considered. I have already given a negative answer to this question. The question I am now asking is whether people of integrity can *sometimes* fall short of living the full set of values they profess.

Here is an example. Imagine a woman who is employed by an agency committed to working for the good of the community. Suppose her all-things-considered values would have her work for the good of the community even when this is at odds with acting for personal gain. An occasion arises when she puts her own interest above that of the community. (Perhaps she falsifies information about the potential dangers of the community's water supply to make another worker look bad, thereby increasing her chances for a promotion.) This proves to be an uncharacteristic break in her work ethic, however, and the next day finds her again working for the good of the community, something she continues to do for the rest of her life. What should we say? Is her one failing sufficient to show that she lacks moral integrity?

To answer this question, we must determine whether integrity is an all-or-nothing concept. Some concepts are; others are not. Virginity is an all-or-nothing concept. We cannot be more or less a virgin, and once we have had sexual intercourse, virginity has been lost forever. We cannot become a virgin again. If integrity is like virginity, then people cannot have more or less integrity, and a single lapse in acting in accordance with one's all-things-considered values would mean that one has completely lost one's integrity, never to be regained again.

It is doubtful that integrity is in the same conceptual category as virginity. Two possible analyses support this suspicion. The first begins by noting that the word *integrity* applied in nonmoral contexts suggests a difference. For example, we speak of the integrity of instruments, engines, and gaskets. When we speak of, say, the integrity of a gasket, we mean that it is whole, intact, and functioning properly. If something goes wrong and a gasket begins to leak, its integrity is lost. If it is later repaired and the leak stopped, we say that the integrity of the gasket has been restored. If moral integrity behaves in the same way, then people can violate their integrity on some occasions and reclaim or restore it later. In this respect integrity would be unlike virginity. Expressed another way, the wholeness, the "harmony of the soul," that characterizes people of integrity can be fractured or rendered dissonant by some of the things they do and restored to wholeness or harmony by others. Granted, people who never violate or compromise their all-things-considered values (if, indeed, there are such people) differ from those who sometimes do so. Nonetheless, people who never violate their moral integrity arguably are not the only people of moral integrity.

A second, dispositional analysis of integrity supports this same finding. On this analysis, people who have integrity are disposed to act in ways that exemplify their moral wholeness, the unified set of their values, all things considered. Being disposed to behave in certain ways, however, no more guarantees that one will behave that way in each and every situation than having the dispositional property of being brittle guarantees that a dropped glass will always break. If this is the correct way to view integrity—as a disposition to behave in certain ways—then people do not lose their integrity when they act contrary to their all-things-considered values on one or a few occasions, just as, by analogy, a glass remains brittle (retains the dispositional property to break) even if it sometimes remains intact when dropped.

The two ways of viewing integrity certainly differ. On the first view, people lose their integrity by acting contrary to their all-things-considered values on just a single occasion. On the second view, where integrity is understood as a disposition, integrity is not lost by occasional moral lapses. Which (if either) analysis is correct, I do not know. I wish only to suggest that both are plausible and that both support an important feature of the logic of integrity. Even if it is the first and not the second that should be accepted, integrity, unlike virginity, need not be lost forever by one's failure to uphold one's all-things-considered values on all occasions. Like a leaky gasket, and in this respect unlike virginity, integrity is something that can be restored or regained.

Moral Integrity and Work

When it comes to moral integrity in the workplace, in the employment context, the primary question concerns the demands of our jobs and our all-things-considered values. For those who truly hold the values they espouse, remaining in a job whose demands conflict with their values can cost them their moral integrity.

The frequency of conflicts between people's central values and the circumstances of their employment is anyone's guess. My guess is that it occurs more often than we might suspect. After all, businesses and institutions often engage in practices that would challenge even a modestly developed moral sensibility. As employees, our predicament is complicated by the fact that many of us work for companies or institutions that are anything but simple. Although our jobs themselves may not assault our all-things-con-sidered values, the companies or institutions for which we work might have financial ties to other companies or institutions whose practices do.

The temptation to ignore or minimize such conflicts is all too human. No one wants to think that the blood of what we find unconscionable stains the wages we earn. We all run the risk of Sartrean bad faith when it comes to making moral sense of our actions as employees or, for that matter, em-ployers. For the great majority of us, keeping both our jobs and our moral integrity arguably is not an impossible task, but for all of us, retaining both is probably more difficult than we might find it comfortable to imagine. Still, if the preceding is at least near the truth, integrity, while it is something we can lose as a result of the work we do, is also something we can regain— though possibly not without a struggle.

INDEX

Abelson, Philip H., 31
Academic freedom, 161, 162
Advocacy: logical sense of, 153, 156; normative sense of, 153, 154, 155, 156, 159, 161; political sense of, 154–55, 156, 159, 161, 162
African Americans, 110, 111–16
American Medical Association, 126, 157
American Psychiatric Association, 125, 126
American Society for Value Inquiry, 39, 40
Ammon, Pastor William H., 129
Animal rights, 35–36, 38, 100–103; abolition and, 18, 19; amorality rights argument against, 76–78; community argument against, 80–83; contrasted with animal welfare, 142–43; debate over, 2, 23; deep ecology and, 19–21; ecofeminism and, 21–22; feminist indictment of, 53–64; importance of, 72; movement, 28, 40, 141–48; predation problem and, 19; right-kind argument against, 78–80; violence and, 139, 140, 145–49. *See also* Rights view
Animals: cruelty to, 8, 12, 13, 30–32, 33; exclusion from moral community, 127–36; liberation of, 36–38; predation problem and, 19; psychology of, 3, 6, 73; in research, 15–16, 18, 19, 71, 72, 103–4; as subject of a life, 17, 43, 48, 49, 50, 98, 101; welfare of, 33–35, 134, 142–43
Animal Welfare Act, 1, 134
Animal Welfare Caucus, 157
Antislavery movement, 143–48
Appeal to intuitions, 44–47
Applied ethics, 152, 153, 154, 155
Aquinas, St. Thomas, 8, 13, 73

Aristotle, 5–7, 8, 13, 24, 61, 129
Armstrong, George D., 111–12, 113, 116

Baltimore, David, 130, 131
Bentham, Jeremy, 13, 14, 17, 67
Bioethics, 1, 2
Bradley, F. H., 73
Brown, John, 146, 148
Brownson, Orestes A., 119–20, 135
Buettinger, Craig, 133, 134
Burr, Chandler, 125

Calvin, John, 128
Carruthers, Peter, 73
Cartwright, Samuel, 115
Christianity: "sin model" of homosexuality and, 121–23; used in defending slavery, 111–13; used in defending subjugation of women, 119–20; used in excluding animals from moral community, 7–8, 127–28
Clark, Edward H., 120, 135
Cohen, Carl, 66–84
Coleman, R. R., 120–21, 135
Contractarianism, 9–12, 23
Cruelty to animals, 8, 12, 13, 30–32, 33

Dana, Charles Loomis, 1, 133, 134
Darwin, Charles, 94
DeCyon, Elie, 132–33
Deep ecology, 19–21, 22, 23. *See also* Animal rights
Dennis, Clarence, 134
Descartes, René, 3, 6, 129, 130
Despotism, 7–9, 23
Devall, Bill, 20, 21, 22

Tom Regan is a professor of philosophy and a University Alumni Distinguished Professor at North Carolina State University, where he has taught for more than thirty years. His more than twenty books include *The Case for Animal Rights* (1983), *Bloomsbury's Prophet: G. E. Moore and the Development of His Moral Philosophy* (1987), and *The Thee Generation: Reflections on the Coming Revolution* (1991).

Typeset in 10/13 Janson
with Officina Serif display
Designed by Paula Newcomb
Composed by Celia Shapland
for the University of Illinois Press
Manufactured by Thomson-Shore, Inc.

University of Illinois Press
1325 South Oak Street
Champaign, IL 61820-6903
www.press.uillinois.edu